BITTER WEEDS
AND
BURNING BUSHES

WILLIAM J. LACY

BROADMAN PRESS
NASHVILLE, TENNESSEE

© Copyright 1990 • Broadman Press
All rights reserved
4250-94
ISBN: 0-8054-5094-7
Dewey Decimal Classification: 248.4
Subject Heading: CHRISTIAN LIFE
Library of Congress Catalog Card Number: 90-30022
Printed in the United States of America

Unless otherwise indicated, all quotations of the Scripture are from the *New American Standard Bible. Copyright © The Lockman Foundation, 1960, 1962, 1963, 1971, 1972, 1973, 1975, 1977. Used by permission.*

Library of Congress Cataloging-in-Publication Data

Lacy, William J., 1933-
    Bitter weeds and burning bushes / William J. Lacy.
        p.   cm.
    Includes bibliographical references.
    ISBN 0-8054-5094-7
    1. Christian life—Anecdotes.   2. Christian life—Baptist authors.
3. Lacy, William, J., 1933.   I. Title.
BV4517.L33   1990
286'.1'092—dc20
[B]

90-30022
CIP

To
Mary Ruth Lacy
whose life is a prayer

Preface

"Welcome to Superworld. We never close." Such words could be emblazoned on planet earth which is not so alive or well. On staff at Superworld are Superman, Superwoman, Superboy, and Supergirl. On our front pages are superpowers. In our arsenals are super weapons. On our oceans are super tankers. We buy our groceries at supermarkets. A climactic event of our year is the Super Bowl. The game may be played in the Super Dome. We make idols, as well as millionares, of superstars. On Babylon Boulevard, an unadvertised special is super sin.

As a part of our superholic fixation we have super churches, super Sundays, super saints, and super sermons. We worship at the shrine of the spectacular. If it is not bigger and better, it is boring. Our craving for the sensational is *sinsational*. A causalty of our day is the idea that God can speak through the ordinary, through the common ventures of life, through plain-vanilla, unvarnished people.

God speaks with a thousand tongues. He may not speak with a larynx and vocal chords, but He speaks. Only God should be classified as "the" great communicator. God spoke to Adam in the cool of the garden. He spoke to Noah through a flood, to Balaam through a donkey, to Jacob when he slept with stones for a pillow, to Isaiah through a vision in the temple, to Jeremiah through a boiling pot, to Ezekiel through a valley of dry bones, to Daniel through a dream, to Hosea through his marital problems, and to Jonah through a profound need.

God speaks through the Bible, through a sermon, through a godly life, through a song, and through a tragedy. God speaks through His created universe. The psalmist (Ps. 19:1) sang:

> The heavens are telling of the glory of God;
> And their expanse is declaring the work of His hands.

Paul shared a similar insight in Romans 1:20, "For the invisible things of him from the creation of the world are clearly seen, being understood by the things that are made, even his eternal power and Godhead; so that they are without excuse."

God has spoken to me. I have not heard a voice as did Samuel. I have not stood on any Mount of Transfiguration. A hand writing on the wall has not appeared to me. The Damascus Road has never been my address. I have never been caught up to the third heaven. Neither have I heard the seraphim cry out about the holiness of God.

My cleft of the rock, where I have seen the back side of the glory of God, has been in the common experiences of life. By the grace of God, the ordinary has become extraordinary. These pages chronicle the discovery that God speaks to each of us through daily life experiences. In the chapters that follow I shall interpret Scripture, and I apply it to the contemporary scene through utilizing numerous experiences during my early years in my home state. The life setting for appropriating several deep truths is Lauderdale County, Mississippi. I have learned that God can also speak through bushes which are not burning. A spiritual rendezvous can occur at wells other than Jacob's. Jesus calms storms at addresses other than Galilee. To recognize this requires insight described by Blake which enables one:

> To see a World in a grain of sand,
> And a Heaven in a wild flower,
> Hold Infinity in the palm of your hand,
> And Eternity in an hour.[1]

Francis Thompson was gifted with this special vision in writing:

> The angels keep their ancient places:—
> Turn but a stone, and start a wing!
> 'Tis ye, 'tis your estranged faces,
> That miss the many-splendoured thing.[2]

PREFACE

Multitudes of the choicest folks on earth, of all races, are in Mississippi. Many of my relatives still live in the area where I was reared. Mississippi is a beautiful state. If the Lord had had second thoughts about the location for the Garden of Eden, He would have put it at the junction of the Mississippi and the Yazoo rather than the Tigris and Euphrates. The course of man's history might have been more enlightened. The ancestors of Huckleberry Finn could have dealt with snakes better than did Adam and Eve.

These pages will involve a reflection on my roots, physical and spiritual. My list of "begats" includes Lacys, McDonalds, Culpeppers, and Hardins, humble, hard-working folks who have left a goodly heritage and helped the lines of life fall to me in pleasant places.

Through the months of writing and review, my wife, Mary Ruth, has been my Aaron and Hur. She has been my inspirer and wise critic. My secretary, Mrs. Myrna Carter, has rendered second-mile service in manuscript preparation and proof reading. My friend Joe McNeill, Head Cataloger at the McNeese State University Library, has helped immeasurably in verifying details about sources and helping me find books. My mother taught me to say "thank you" for a kindness received. I have received light from many lamps. For each one, thank you.

Contents

Bitter Weeds and
Burning Bushes

1

Praying Between the Plow Handles

Not eloquence, but honesty, reality, awareness of need, communication with God—these are the ingredients of prayer.—William J. Lacy

Introduction

My daddy's name was Les Lacy. His full name was Marvin Lesler Lacy, but everyone called him Les. Daddy had six brothers and three sisters, making ten Lacy children. I assure you, a person would have had to signal for a fair catch to get a biscuit at the Lacy table.

Daddy grew up on a farm in the eastern part of Lauderdale County, Mississippi. The Lacy farm, though small, actually crossed the state line into Alabama. The Lacys lived at the end of a dirt road, and at times the roads left much to be desired. Daddy used to comment that when it rained, you couldn't even fly over the roads in an airplane.

All of his adult life, Daddy worked in sawmills, but he grew up on a farm. When Daddy married my Mother, they bought a small farm in the Alamucha community, on the Old Wire Road, not many miles from where my Daddy was born and within sight of the farm of my mother's parents.

Years ago, Daddy and I were talking about prayer, and he said, "The most beautiful prayer I ever heard was when I walked up to the edge of a field where a black man was plowing, and I found him on his knees, between the plow handles, praying."

For Daddy to make such a statement was quite significant. He heard many pray, including yours truly, others in his family, and numerous preachers and missionaries. A man, on his knees in a field, praying between the plow handles, can be a parable, effectively teaching us some precious lessons about prayer.

The Primacy of Prayer

We learn the primacy of prayer. In politics there are primaries. In the spiritual life there are also primaries. All of us of every age need to enroll in the spiritual primary department.

Primary among institutions is the church; primary among books is the Bible; primary among days is the Lord's day, Sunday; primary among moneys is the tithe. Primary among services is the winning of souls; among loyalties, our loyalty to God, among privileges, the privilege of prayer. Primary among primaries is prayer. That is why Paul wrote, "Pray without ceasing" (1 Thess. 5:17). S. D. Gordon advised, "You can do more than pray, after you have prayed. But you cannot do more than pray until you have prayed."[1]

Prayer had preeminent importance for Jesus. Jesus was reared in a Godly home (Luke 2:22-52; 4:16). The practice in His home could well have included three times for prayer: (1) a morning prayer at sunrise, (2) an afternoon prayer at the time when the afternoon sacrifice was offered in the temple, and (3) an evening prayer at night before going to bed.

During His ministry such regularly scheduled occasions for prayer were not enough. One of the many amazing facts about the amazing Christ is the amount of time the perfect Son of God spent in prayer. He prayed at His baptism (Luke 3:21), at the close of His first day of ministry in Capernaum (Mark 1:35-38), in response to multitudes who came to be healed (Luke 5:15-16), before He chose the twelve apostles (Luke 6:12), before and after feeding the five thousand (Matt. 14:13-21; Mark 6:46), at the grave of Lazarus (John 11:41), at the Transfiguration (Luke 9:29), after the Seventy returned (Luke 10:21), before He taught the disciples His Model Prayer (Luke 11:1), after leaving the Upper Room as He prayed the High Priestly prayer (John 17:1-26), in the Garden of

Gethsemane (Matt. 26:36-46), for the stedfastness of Simon Peter (Luke 22:31-32), and on the cross. Jesus prayed about the cross (John 12:27-28), and three of His seven sayings from the cross were prayers.

"Father forgive them; for they do not know what they are doing" (Luke 23:34) was a prayer for His enemies. "My God, My God, why hast Thou forsaken Me?" (Mark 15:34) was a cry of dereliction and a quotation of Psalm 22:1, indicating that Jesus was probably meditating on the entire psalm. "Father, into Thy hands I commit My Spirit" (Luke 23:46) was a quotation of Psalm 31:5 which was a bed-time prayer that Jewish mothers taught their children.

The only *recorded* time of Jesus' sweating was when He prayed. Except for the quotation of Psalm 22:1 from the cross, all the prayers of Jesus address God as Father, and the word *Abba* was used. Other than by Jesus, this particular word was not used in Jewish prayers of the first millennium AD. It is a word coming from the language of children. Joachim Jeremias concludes, "A new way of praying is born. Jesus talks to His Father as naturally, as intimately, and with the same sense of security as a child talks to his father."[2] I always called my father "daddy." If I had called him "Father," he would have suspected that I was in bad trouble. With others, the word "father" might be very intimate and personal, but not in the familial atmosphere in which I was reared. By using the word *Abba*, Jesus was addressing God as "Daddy."

Prime-time television has its key programs. Prime time Christianity must have the Christ program, and vital to that is prayer. Prayer is primary.

E. F. Hallock reminds us that the Bible is permeated with prayer.[3] There is no definition of prayer in the Bible, and there are no sermons about prayer in the Bible, but it is assumed that men and women must and will pray. There are invitations, exhortations, and commands to pray. As the Bible is permeated with prayer, so the Christian life must be permeated with prayer.

Charles G. Finney told about a woman who was afraid her husband would pray himself to death.[4] I have known men whom I feared might work themselves to death. I have feared others might worry themselves to death. I have never known a person whom I feared might pray himself to death!

The Principles of Prayer

Praying in a field between plow handles is not choosing an ordinary closet, but the one praying there has recognized certain valid principles of prayer. He has chosen the *right place* in that it was private. For the deepest experiences, the prayer office will be a private office. The man praying was not aware that my dad was anywhere around. We pray with prayer partners, with families, with churches, and nations, but the most intimate praying is private, secret prayer. It is difficult to draw aside from children, telephones, and television, but each of us needs a corner, a chair, a table that can become an altar. John Oxenham described it as:

> A little place of mystic grace,
>   Of self and sin swept bare,
> Where I may look upon Thy face,
>   And talk with Thee in prayer.[5]

The worker chose the *right posture*. He kneeled. Kneeling can be a way to get in good standing with God. There are several correct postures, but surely kneeling is one of them. Mark 11:25 mentions those who pray standing. David prayed while sitting (2 Sam. 7:18). In Gethsemane, Jesus fell prostrate and prayed lying down. Hezekiah turned his face to the wall and prayed (Isa. 38:2). At times George Whitefield would lie all day prostrate in prayer. Elie Wiesel, a survivor of the concentration camps at Auschwitz and Buchenwald has written about a Rabbi Mikhal of Zlotchev who used to pray knocking his head against a wall until he drew blood.[6]

Fervent prayers have been offered while one was lying flat on his back in a hospital bed. On Monday, November 10, 1986, I visited Fred Mc-Clure in St. Patrick's Hospital (Lake Charles, Louisiana) shortly before he was taken to have surgery on his hip. Fred had been a long-time deacon in the First Baptist Church of Lake Charles. Even in years of declining health, he had been extremely faithful to his church.

In the room at the time of my visit were some members of his family, Mrs. McClure, Mr. and Mrs. Earl Swain, Sr., and Earl Swain, Jr. For several days Brother Fred had been quite weak, his voice scarcely more than a whisper. During the visit, Mrs. Swain, Sr., related that a few days before, while her dad had been in bed in his weakened condition, he had suddenly begun to pray. He prayed with a strong and distinct voice for about two minutes. Mrs. Swain thought her dad had imagined that he was in church and had been called on to pray. Neither his posture nor his poor health minimized the faith of a praying deacon.

When we kneel, we recognize One greater than we, and the choirs of our egos quit singing "How Great I Am." When we kneel we crucify pride. There are more than seven deadly sins. All sin is deadly, but the deadliest is pride. During World War II, Edward R. Murrow reported from England, "In the autumn of 1940 when Britain stood alone, when the bombers came at dusk each evening and went away at dawn, I observed a sign on a church just off the East India Dock Road; it was crudely lettered and it read, 'If your knees knock, kneel on them.'"[7]

The friend kneeling between the plow handles prayed for the right purpose. T. S. Eliot was right:

> The last temptation is the greatest treason:
> To do the right deed for the wrong reason.[8]

There are many wrong ways to do what is right, and the end does not justify ungodly means. In many ways we pollute what is pure. We pollute our water and our air. We use liberty for license, literature for lust, and government for greed.

We abuse prayer. Manipulators kneel to pray. If we look upon prayer as an attempt to make God see things our way, we have abused it. The very opposite should be true. Prayer is our effort to see things God's way. If prayer becomes a Pharisaical ego trip, we have our reward, but it is not God's reward. If prayer becomes our means of getting enough names on a petition so God will be obligated to vote our way, we have abused prayer. If prayer is viewed as magic so at our prayer benches we can leave our further responsibilities, as well as our burdens, we have distorted prayer. If prayer is seen only as an aid to our devotional lives—and I am often tempted to so regard it—we have abused prayer, and we are spiritual manipulators.

Our purpose is to find God and to become instruments of His will. Anything less is a waste.

The Perspective of Prayer

The plowman kneeling in the dirt had the right perspective about prayer. Thomas Brooks recognized the importance of proper perspective in stating:

> God looks not at the oratory of your prayers, how elegant they may be; nor at the geometry of your prayers, how long they may be; nor at the arithmetic of your prayers, how many they may be; nor at the logic of your prayers, how methodical they may be; but the sincerity of them he looks at.[9]

His prayer would have been simple. We can use the kiss, K-I-S-S, formula in praying: "keep it simple, stupid." I read an interesting story about Dr. John Duncan who was an outstanding theologian. He knew the Hebrew language proficiently. Some of his students wondered whether he spoke in Hebrew when he prayed. One day two students listened discreetly outside his door at his prayer time. Rather than hearing the diction of Hebrew parallelism, they heard the simple words:

> Gentle Jesus, meek and mild,
> Look upon a little child,
> Pity my simplicity,
> Suffer me to come to Thee.[10]

James Montgomery was to the point in writing:

> Prayer is the simplest form of speech
> That infant lips can try;
> Prayer the sublimest strains that reach
> The majesty on high.[11]

The plowman's prayer would have been personal. He was not casually "dialing a deity" or thinking of "Somebody up there who likes me." He was not trying to contact a first cause or moral absolute or ground of all being. His was no computerized confession. God is personal, and we are wise to think of Him in personal terms.

The plowman's prayer would have been direct. Prayer is a direct action program. One need not go around the world to cross the street. One does not need arbitrators, negotiators, or any other third parties. Each of us is a priest, and ours is the privilege of direct access. When the sun is causing the starch to run out of your shirt, and the sweat is running into your brogans, your prayer will not be circuitous. William Holmes Borders, a great pastor in Atlanta, Georgia, told of hearing an elderly man pray:

> Lord, this little William talking to you,
> You know me better that I know myself, and
>   I know you.
> But I want to be sure I got the main line.[12]

Prayer is not auto-suggestion or self therapy. It is a direct encounter with the living God. Karl Barth observed, "Prayer is not prayer if it is addressed to anyone else but God."[13]

The prayer in the field would have been specific. He was not praying for all the missionaries and all the sick. He had something definite on his mind. What our world needs is spirituality in specifics, not abstractions.

A minister was surprised after church one Sunday morning when a lady in his congregation asked him to pray for her gall bladder. He replied that it was not his habit to be quite so specific in his prayers.

"Oh, but you are!" she exclaimed. "Why, just last week you prayed for all the loose livers."

Farmers like the story about the new hen who came to the hen house and spoke to the head rooster. The hen said, "I am about to lay my first egg, and I want to lay it in a dramatic way. Could I lay it on your back?"

The rooster replied, "No, that has been tried."

"Could I lay it on the top of a fence post?" asked the hen.

"Someone tried that last week," answered the rooster.

"Could I lay it on the roof of the hen house?" continued the hen.

"We have that all the time," replied the rooster.

The hen paused to think and asked, "Could I lay it on the interstate highway?"

The rooster responded, "OK, but lay it on the line and do it quickly!"

In prayer, we need to lay it on the line. We need to be specific. Charles Schulz's comic strip character, Lucy, says, "I love mankind. It's people I can't stand."[14]

My dad described the prayer in the field as beautiful. Beautiful in what way? I doubt if he meant beautiful in grammar. Quite likely it was not impressive in its vocabulary. Its inspiration would be questionable because of its lack of logical arrangement. It would not have been distinguished by its inflection or elocution. In his *Church Dogmatics,* Barth wrote of prayer:

> It does not have to be beautiful or edifying, logically coherent or theologically correct. Neither formally, materially nor methodically does it have to display any kind of art. Its formation can be determined only by its own inner law.[15]

Barth affirmed that if one can only sigh, stammer, and mutter in prayer, that God will hear, understand it, and accept it as right.

The prayer between the plow handles would have been beautiful in its reality. No games were being played. No masks were worn. Nothing was counterfeit. It was a genuine moment of reality. Prayer should not become a trip to Fantasy Island. Unlike the mule he was plowing, the man between the plow handles would not have been wearing blinders. A Christian can easily put on spiritual blinders and find himself insulated and anesthetized against pains of poverty, loneliness, and despair. Johann Baptist Metz has written, "With our back toward Auschwitz we prayed and celebrated our liturgy. Only later I began to ask myself what kind of religion it is that can be practised unmoved by such a catastrophe."[16] When we pray with our backs toward Auschwitz, we pray with our backs toward God.

The prayer was beautiful in its truth. Frequently we fear the truth.

How refreshing are moments of basic, sometimes even brutal, honesty.

The prayer was beautiful in its encounter. The furrow was a divine-human rendezvous. The plowman and the Lord of the harvest did not pass each other in the darkness. This prayer would not have been like the one prayed by Jacob at Bethel, lamenting the fact that God had been present, and he had known it. The plowman used no vain repetitions. His prayer was not a broken record. James Russell Lowell reflected:

> I that still pray at morning and at eve . . .
> Thrice in my life perhaps have truly prayed,
> Thrice, stirred below my conscious self, have felt
> That perfect disenthralment which is God.[17]

Sometimes we pray, and, as with Isaiah, the foundations shake and the seraphim take wings to fly.

Following his prayer, the plowman went to work. So should it always be with prayer. E. M. Bounds described prayer as the most serious work of our most serious years.[18] Prayer is not an escape but a refueling. It is not a change of address to an ivory tower, but, a reporting for duty to serve as an ambassador for Christ. Prayer itself is hard work. Following prayer we put feet to our prayers. God answers many of our own prayers through us. The poet put it well:

> You must use your hands while praying, though,
>   If an answer you would get;
> For prayer-worn knees and a rusty hoe
>   Never raised a big crop yet.[19]

The Power of Prayer

In the plowman who took a break so many years ago, we see the primacy of prayer; some principles of prayer; the perspective of prayer, and the power of prayer. I do not know what happened in the plowman's life following his prayer. I do not know what changed, what miracle occurred, what healing took place, but I do know this: in a nuclear age, the most powerful force on earth is the power of prayer. I do not make such a statement glibly in the spirit of a man whistling through the cemetery. I have prayed for many people to get well, and some of them did not recover. I have prayed for numerous things to happen, and some of them did not come to pass according to my blueprint. I have learned this: God uses praying men and women, and when we pray, miracles happen, and other things occur which may not qualify as miraculous, but they would never have transpired without prayer.

S. D. Gordon noted there are five outlets of power in the Christian life: one's total life, what one speaks, service, money, and prayer.[20] "The greatest of these" is prayer. Gordon wrote of those who pray:

> These are the people today who are doing the most for God; in winning souls; in solving problems; in awakening churches; in supplying both men and money for mission posts; in keeping fresh and strong these lives far off in sacrificial service on the foreign field where the thickest fighting is going on; in keeping the old earth sweet awhile longer.[21]

A major reason for a power failure in our lives is the neglect of prayer. My aunt, Reba Lacy, was in New York City one night in the summer of 1977 when there occurred a massive power failure. She and a friend were staying on the eighteenth floor of a hotel near Madison Square Garden. They were attending a play when, around nine to nine-thirty in the evening, the power failed. They were plunged into total darkness. At first everyone thought the failure would be temporary, but they were disappointed. After a wait of about thirty minutes they left the theater where the only meager light came from flashlights. In the street the only lights emanated from automobiles.

Subways had no power. Most restaurants were unable to provide meals. Elevators could not function in the hotels. Reba said that guests filled all the chairs in the lobby of her hotel and that many sat on the floor for a few hours, hoping they would not have to walk up the stairs to their rooms. Again, their hopes were fruitless. Late at night Reba walked the eighteen floors to her room. The next morning the city was still powerless, and she walked down eighteen floors.

Those who take God for granted rather than with gratitude will have a power failure. The plays, dreams, plans of their lives will not go as scheduled. They will sit in darkness. They will walk the floors of life in darkness. Prayer is the switch that turns on the light.

Praying "Between"

The plowman prayed between the plow handles. We need some "between" praying today.

Let us, like Jesus, pray between crosses, understanding our crosses to be our personal responsibilities. As Frederick L. Knowles affirmed:

> Our crosses are hewn from different trees,
> But we all must have our calvaries.[22]

Let us pray between the crises. Crisis is normal, and normalcy is abnormal. Crises are economic, political, military, marital, environmental, and spiritual. Prayer brings Christ to the crisis. He specializes not only in damage control but in divine control.

Let us pray between challenges. God's people are challenged to change the world, and about all we are doing is changing channels.

Let us pray between cancers, between physical tumors, and spiritual malignancies for which the only cure is Christ-therapy.

Let us pray between catastrophes. We pray between holocausts, between the holocaust that was Auschwitz and the holocaust of Armageddon.

Let us pray between causes. Spiritually, some play Trivial Pursuit, and others find causes worth living for and worth dying for. If you don't have a cause, find a cause. If you don't have a leader, be one.

Let us pray between cheapnesses. We cheapen life with abortion on demand, and we cheapen the gospel by presenting a bargain-basement Christianity. Prayer affirms values beyond estimate.

Let us pray between choices. Life is a series of unavoidable choices. We choose our friends. We choose our work. We choose whether or not to continue education. We choose which car to buy and which house to purchase. We choose heaven or hell, and if Christ is to be ours, and we are to pray without ceasing, then it is Christ whom we must choose.

2

A Night in the Storm Pit

"Then the Lord answered Job out of the whirlwind."—Job 40:6

Introduction

My first home was in a rural area of Lauderdale County, Mississippi. We lived in the Alamucha community, the general area where my mother and daddy were reared. My daddy worked in saw mills. Shortly after I was born, we moved to Alabama. In subsequent years we moved to Georgia and South Carolina, before we moved back to Lauderdale County and Meridian, Mississippi, when I was sixteen years of age.

During my early years, each summer my mother and daddy would send me back to Mississippi to visit relatives for about a month (my folks probably craved some peace and quiet).

My mother's parents were named McDonald. My grandfather's name was Brantley Judson McDonald. My middle name is Judson as I am named after my two granddaddys. My "Paw Paw" McDonald spent plenty of time with me during those brief visits. He would take me fishing in the Bell Branch. He took me squirrel hunting. He "let" me pick just enough cotton for me to know there is a pretty close resemblance between picking cotton and work. I can appreciate the man who was about halfway down a long cotton row one hot summer day when he paused and prayed, "Lord, this row is so long and the sun is so hot, I believe I have been called to preach."

My grandparents' large house was built out of lumber. The house must have stood four feet off the ground. In those days kids could have a big time playing under the house. The house had a roomy yard, front and back. My grandmother had a lot of flowers. Granddaddy never had to cut the grass. They didn't allow grass to grow in the yard. If a sprig of grass sprouted, they got rid of it.

Near the back of their house was the smoke house. They could kill hogs, put the meat in boxes of salt and smoke the hams. In the vernacular of Jerry Clower, it was "fit to eat." Back of the smoke house were the chicken house and chicken yard. To the right of that was the barn and lot, and back of the chicken yard was the garden.

Some distance from the garden, in the edge of a field, was a shelter called a storm pit. I don't know if all country people in the 1930s and 1940s did or not, but my grandparents had a healthy respect for the weather. If they had heard that a hurricane was coming, they would not have driven to the coast for a hurricane party. They had a storm pit, and they used it. The storm pit was basically a hole in the ground, with dirt floor and sides, with a top covered with tin about level with the ground.

One of the oldest memories I have is of being waked up in the middle of the night at my grandparents' home. In those old feather mattresses, it probably required an Eagle Scout to find me. Waking me up, they led me to the storm pit where we spent the rest of the night while a storm raged outside.

The Storms of Life

I want us to learn from a man who became a veteran in storm pits. Actually, his storm pits were rather limited. He was directly exposed to the storms. The man's name was Job. What were some storms that blew through his life? One was a storm of *economic adversity*. Job had 7,000 sheep, 3,000 camels, 500 yoke of oxen, 500 donkeys, and many servants (Job 1:3). He lost them all in one day. He was completely wiped out. Job would have remembered the day as "Black Monday" or black whatever day it was. His futures market became a disaster area.

In the 1980s, economic adversity was a frequent visitor to some parts of the United States. Numerous farmers have lost their farms. Bank failures have increased. Oil companies have cut back. Automobile assembly plants are being closed. Bankruptcy courts are busy. Some churches are offering employment counsel. I visited with a couple who was having economic adversity. The wife told me she read the psalms all the time. Job could sympathize with hard times. He had them.

A second storm was the storm of *disease*. Job was soon covered with boils from head to toe (Job 2:7). He was so disfigured that when his friends first saw him, they did not recognize him (Job 2:12). Doctors might well study Job's symptoms and diagnose his case. Job 7:5 reads, "My flesh is clothed with worms and a crust of dirt;/my skin hardens and runs." Job 19:20 indicates, "My bone clings to my skin and my flesh,/And I have escaped only by the skin of my teeth." In Job 30:30, Job grieved, "My skin turns black on me,/and my bones burn with fever." Sooner or later most of us will see the wrinkled brow of a physician, and a storm of disease will blow through our lives. Most people pass through Baca. They certainly come to Baca. Passing through is not a certainty.

As Job learned much from his suffering, so too can we. There is much wisdom in the lines by Robert B. Hamilton:

> I walked a mile with pleasure,
> She chatted all the way
> But left me none the wiser
> For all she had to say.
>
> I walked a mile with sorrow
> And never a word said she
> But Oh! The things I learned from her
> When sorrow walked with me.[1]

Suffering *can* be a great teacher. It is not automatically a great teacher. If you doubt that, the next time you drop a log on your foot, ask yourself how much more saintly you have become. When you wake up at two o'clock in the morning with a toothache, ask yourself how readily your mind turns to the things of God. I have visited many sick people, and not very many looked upon their affliction as an opportunity for spiritual growth.

Paul's thorn in the flesh led to his confidence in the grace sufficient. John's exile on Patmos was the home of visions that few if any others have ever seen. Many of life's greatest achievements have come from blind Miltons, deaf Beethovens, and imprisoned Bunyans. The blood of the martyrs did become the seed of church.

There is nothing certain, however, about suffering being a boost for sanctification. David Ray, a Texas evangelist, says, "Hurts can make you bitter or make you better."[2] Many of us know folks whom hurts have made bitter. Some members of churches have not darkened the door of the church in years because of some tragedy for which they blamed God. Many things happen which are *not* the will of God, but God is often blamed for them.

Job was part of a theological storm. Satan made a personal test case of Job. He gave Job his undivided attention. Satan went into his two-minute offense and used every device and every trick in the book to hang Job on the wall as his trophy. Job was at the eye of the storm.

Job lived in a day when the popular theology concluded that if a person suffered, it was because he had sinned. Basically, Job's friends said to him, "Job, confess your sins, and you will get well." The Book of Job is in the Bible to combat that kind of theology. Many Christians do not have a sound theology of suffering. Some have become disenchanted because an illness or accident struck them personally or a loved one, and they could not deal with it. They believe like Eliphaz, Zophar, and Bildad, that if a person loves God, everything is always rosy.

Job lived in a day when many believed life after death was an existence in a place, where there was only shadowy, minimal existence and not the joyful celebration that we anticipate in heaven. Job had a pioneering faith (Job 19:25) in expressing confidence in a living Redeemer who would vindicate him after death.

Every generation has theological storms. Jesus had them. The apostles had them. The churches at Corinth, Ephesus, and Pergamum had them. Twentieth-century churches are having them. The storms may be over charismatic movements, ecumenical movements, new age movements, old age movements, parachurch organizations, televangelism, the question of authority, the nature of the Bible, the ordination of women, manipulative politics, new moralities, responses to social concerns about issues such as race relations, abortion, and illegal drugs. The winds of divers doctrines always blow. There is a constant flow of new movements, new discoveries, new scholarship, new progress, new isms, new heresies.

One must always try the spirits, distinguish false prophets from the true prophets, and sift the good from the bad. Our challenge is found in Paul's admonition (1 Thess. 5:21), "But examine everything carefully; hold fast to that which is good."

Job sailed his ship into a storm of loneliness. Job had ten children, seven sons and three daughters, and they were all killed the same hour. What do you say to someone who has lost ten children? When Job's three "friends" did come to visit him, they sat for seven days before they spoke a word.

In the midst of his heartache, Job's wife urged ". . . curse God and die!" (Job 2:9). Job lamented, "I am a joke to my friends" (12:4). Job protested to his friends, "But you smear with lies" (13:4). In Job 16:16, he moaned, "My face is flushed from weeping." In Job 19:14, his statement was, "My relatives have failed, / and my intimate friends have forgotten me." He continued to lament, "All my associates abhor me" (Job 19:19). During the writing of this book, a member of our church visited me twice in the same week, weeping profusely in his loneliness.

Dr. Henlee Barnette has written about four kinds of loneliness.[3] *Existential loneliness* is what we all feel at times due to changes such as moving away from friends and familiar places. *Chronic loneliness* is persistent and may contribute to delinquency in adolescents or depression in adults. *Characterological loneliness* stems from character types that tend to steer individuals into risk situations which lead to loneliness. *Ontological loneliness* is the feeling that one is cut off from ultimate reality.

One author has written about what he calls *cosmic loneliness*.[4] In a *Psychology Today* article entitled "The Age of Indifference," Dr. Philip

Zimbardo, a professor of psychology at Stanford University, wrote:

> I know of no more potent killer than isolation. There is no more destructive
> influence on physical and mental health than the isolation of you from me
> and of us from them. It has been shown to be a central agent in the etiology
> of depression, paranoia, schizophrenia, rape, suicide, mass murder . . .[5]

The first thing that God described as "not good" was loneliness (Gen.
2:18).

The storm of loneliness spun off a storm of despair. In Job 3:1, Job
cursed the fact that he was ever born. In Job 6:9, Job asked God to take
his life. In Job 9:21, Job spoke of despising his life. Job cried of his
anguish and of the grave being ready for him. Job's ash heap became the
equivalent of Elijah's juniper tree.

Soren Kierkegaard described despair as a sickness unto death.[6] Its
contemporary symptoms can be seen in our drug culture, the increasing
teen-age suicide rate, spreading occult practices, and various nihilistic
movements.

Despair is not the invention of modern psychology. Under his juniper
tree, Elijah was on the verge of despair. When he was near death the
Duke of Wellington thanked God that he would "be spared from seeing
the consummation of ruin that is gathering around us."[7]

God's Answers in the Storm

In these storms, God spoke to Job. In Job 38:1 we read, "Then the
Lord answered Job out of the whirlwind." Job 40:6 echoes the same
thought. What does God say to him in the storm? He speaks to him about
learning. God asks, "Who is this that darkens counsel / By words without knowledge?" (Job 38:2).

A little learning indeed is a dangerous thing. If we think education is
expensive, let us consider the cost of ignorance. What we don't know
can hurt us. It can kill us! Zeal without knowledge is dangerous. It can
decimate churches and destroy denominations. Good intentions are important, but they are not adequate to provide lasting answers. Harold
Dye, who has worked much with senior adults, says, "We are old when

we quit learning."[8] At the Church of the Savior in Washington D.C., a woman who was practically illiterate joined. Before she died she was a resource leader for the pastor on details in modern theology.[9]

God was saying to Job: "Don't be stupid. Learn something. Through your tears and pain and despair, learn something. Learn something about God. You are only on the outskirts of His ways. Learn something about life after death. There is more to the future life than is dreamt of in your philosophy, Horatio. Learn something about friendship. Bildad, Eliphaz, and Zophar are fair-weather friends. There is a friend who will lay down his life for you. Learn something about patience and prayer and grace."

Jesus said, "Take my yoke upon you and *learn* from Me" (Matt. 11:29). Are we ready to matriculate in His class? The yoke goes with the study.

Out of the whirlwind God spoke to Job about his loins. God said, "Now gird up your loins like a man . . ." (38:3). In Bible times, what was called a girdle was a waistband or belt. It might have been a rope or lengthy cloth which could be wrapped around the waist several times. It could have been a wide leather belt to which there might have been attached a sword, a purse, or a writing case. When a person was working or traveling he might take the ends of his tunic or robe and tuck them into his belt. This was called "girding the loins," and the phrase became an idiom for energetic action.

As God said to Moses and Jeremiah and Job, so He says to us, "Gird up your loins." Be ready. Be one of Gideon's 300. Mobilize your resources. Develop believers. Sound the call to action. Attack. In the spirit of Caleb, let us go up at once and possess the land, for by the grace of God we are well able to overcome it.

> Christians, gird up your loins.
> Councils of deacons, gird up your loins.
> Finance committees, gird up your loins.
> Staff members, gird up your loins.
> Missions committees, gird up your loins.
> Youth, gird up your loins.

Single adults, gird up your loins.
Senior adults, gird up your loins.
Colleges and seminaries, gird up your loins.
Denominational leadership, gird up your loins.

Gird up the loins of your *mind*. God forbid that the world should carry the day because the enemy outthinks us. We need more thinkers. Too often, even when I read and study, I do not properly evaluate what I am reading. I do not ask hard questions and think through implications of what is said. A college freshman who had a speech impediment was called on to pray one night in a dormitory prayer meeting. He intended to pray, "Lord, make us more thankful." Because of his impediment, his words sounded like, "Lord, make us more thinkful."[10] Either way, he prayed a great prayer. We all need to pray, "Lord, make us more thinkful!"

Gird up the loins of your *time*. Yesterday is a cancelled check. Tomorrow is a promissory note. The only time we have is *now*. The imperative stewardship of time is expressed in the lines:

I have only just a minute,
Only sixty seconds in it;
Forced upon me, can't refuse it;
Didn't seek it, didn't choose it;
But it's up to me to use it.

I must suffer if I lose it;
Give account if I abuse it;
Just a tiny little minute;
But eternity is in it.[11]

Gird up the loins of your *attitude*. The longer I live the more important do I regard attitude. It is devastating to pursue right spiritual answers in the wrong way. We are products of our attitudes. A positive, winning, enthusiastic attitude is more than half the battle. A positive attitude is healing as well as heavenly. The *Phillips Modern English Bible* translates Philippians 2:5, "Let your attitude to life be that of Christ Jesus himself." God does not need crepe-hangers. He needs persons who will expect great things from God and attempt great things for Him.

Gird up the loins of your *pocketbook*. We cannot win a world with tips and leftovers. Too many churches have within them UFOs, Uncommitted Freeloading Onlookers. Jack Stack is a splendid deacon in my home church, the Poplar Springs Drive Baptist Church, Meridian, Mississippi. Jack testifies that he made a great discovery when he learned what a joy it was to give away someone else's money. It is all God's money, and money does talk. It says, "Share me to the glory of God."

Gird up the lions of your *prayers*. Prayer is more than words mumbled over a meal or in the twilight zone before sleep. It is our most serious work. A nineteenth-century black spiritual put the message to music:

> I've been in the storm so long,
> You know I've been in the storm so long,
> O Lord, give me more time to pray,
> I've been in the storm so long.

> I am a motherless child,
> Singin' I am a motherless child,
> Singin' Oh Lord, give me more time to pray,
> I've been in the storm so long.

> This is a needy time,
> This is a needy time,
> Singin' Oh Lord, give me more time to pray,
> I've been in the storm so long.

> Lord, I need you now,
> Lord, I need you now,
> Singin' Oh Lord, give me more time to pray,
> I've been in the storm so long.

> My neighbors need you now,
> My neighbors need you now,
> Singin' Oh Lord, give me more time to pray,
> I've been in the storm so long.

> My children need you now,
> My children need you now,

> Singin' Oh Lord, give me more time to pray,
> I've been in the storm so long.
>
> Just look what a shape I'm in,
> Just look what a shape I'm in,
> Crying' Oh Lord, give me more time to pray,
> I've been in the storm so long.[12]

If we are going to gird up our loins, then we cannot be at ease in Zion. Vance Havner quipped that some Christians paraphrase a hymn to read:

> I would be carried to the skies
> On flowery beds of ease;
> Though others fought to win the prize,
> I'm not so hard to please.[13]

Some Christians want a Heavenly Father who is like an indulgent grandfather gifted at spiritually spoiling children. Many are not ready for the discipline involved in loin-girding.

If you want to live life at its best, gird up your loins. Don't endure. Don't exist. Don't live from paycheck to paycheck. Don't let life be a perpetual winter of discontent. It's not the time you put in; it's what you put in the time. George Bernard Shaw noted that the epitaph appearing on many tombstones should be, "Died at thirty, buried at sixty."[14] Christians preach about life after death, and some people wonder if there is life *before* death. John Newton remarked about one person's death, "Tell me not how the man died, but how he lived."[15]

Gird up your loins to walk the hight road of life. John Oxenham described for us the fateful choice that too often leaves the high road "the road not taken."

> To every man there openeth
> A way and ways and a way;
> and the high soul treads the high way
> and the low soul gropes the low;
> and in between on the misty flats
> The rest drift to and fro;
> But to every man there openeth

> a high way and a low;
> And every man decideth
> the way his soul shall go.[16]

As it was to Job, God's Word to us is "Gird up your loins."

God speaks to Job about learning, about his loins being girded. Then He says "listen." That word does not appear in Job 38, but that is what God intends. In Job 38:4, God asks a question, "Where were you when I laid the foundation of the earth?" In the next verse, God asks Job a question in return. God poses questions in Job 38:6, 7, and 8. Job 38:9-11 constitutes one question. God continues to question Job through chapter 38. God says, "Job, you have been doing a lot of talking. Now is the time to listen."

To be an effective pastor, to be a teacher, to be a parent, to be a friend, it is important to listen. Someone should compose a hymn with the title, "O for a Thousand Ears to Hear." Noise pollution comes in many varieties. We crown Christ the Lord of listeners.

To what are we trained to listen? Some are trained to listen to the truth. Some give attention to lies. Others perk up their ears at gossip. A few specialize in scandal. Do twentieth-century Jobs listen to God? In Archibald MacLeish's play, *J.B.*, there are lines where Nickles says:

> Job is everywhere we go,
> His children dead, his work for nothing,
> Counting his losses, scraping his boils,
> Discussing himself with his friends and physicians,
> Questioning everything—the times, the stars,
> His own soul, God's providence.[17]

Job is everywhere we go. He is on Madison Avenue, Wall Street, Broadway, and Pennsylvania Avenue. Paul with his thorn, Elijah with his juniper tree, and the exiles by the River Chebar are multiplied at thousands of addresses today.

Some have ashes for breakfast. They walk a bridge over troubled waters. They load sixteen tons of number-nine coal, and what do they get but another day older and deeper in debt?

Are we tuned to God's wavelength? Can we hear His still, small voice? A tribute was paid to a person with the words:

> His thoughts were slow,
> His words were few, and never formed
> to glisten.
> But he was a joy to all his friends—
> You should have heard him listen.[18]

Years ago in Lagrange, Georgia, there was a preacher who would pause periodically during his sermons and ask, "Are you listening?" Today, as we sit in our storm pits or on our ash heaps and scrape our sores with assorted potsherds, God whispers, "Are you listening?"

3

Bitter Weeds

I do believe, however, that even a cripple can be bigger than anything that can happen to him or her.[1]*—Esther Cathy*

Introduction

In the pastures of Mississippi there grow weeds called "bitter weeds." A bitter weed is stringy and grows to a height of about a foot and has a small, compact, yellow flower. If a dairy cow eats bitter weeds, her milk will taste distinctly bitter.

When I was a boy, we drank our milk just like the Lord and the cow made it. It was neither pasteurized nor homogenized. I can sympathize with the cows who saw a milk truck drive by, and printed in large letters on the truck were the words: "Pasteurized, Homogenized, and Vitamin Enriched." One cow said to the other, "It makes you feel downright inadequate, doesn't it."

Obviously, farmers were anxious for their cows to avoid grazing on bitter weeds. If the cows ate them, the milk would not be palatable. If the milk were to be sold, the bitter weeds would mean a financial loss.

Entirely apart from a rural setting, bitter weeds grow in the pastures of life. We humans eat them, and the result is bitterness. Paul Laurence Dunbar, the gifted poet, had been in touch with some bitter weeds when he wrote:

> A crust of bread and a corner to sleep in,
> A minute to smile and an hour to weep in,
> A pint of joy and a peck of trouble,

> And never a laugh but the moans come double:
> And that is life![2]

On his final birthday, at the age of thirty-six, Lord Byron celebrated with the lines:

> My days are in the yellow leaf;
>   The flowers and fruits of love are gone;
> The worm, the canker, and the grief
>   Are mine alone![3]

In Exodus 15 is the story of Moses' leading the children of Israel in the Exodus. They had entered the Wilderness of Shur. In search of water, they came to Marah where they found a spring, but the water was bitter. After praying for guidance, the Lord led Moses to a tree which Moses threw into the waters, and the waters became sweet.

Fields Where Bitter Weeds Grow

Bitter weeds and bitter waters are on many itineraries. What are some fields where bitter weeds grow? One is the field of our hearts. Like tares they grow with the wheat of life, but unlike tares they must not be left until the harvest. Abuse as a child, discouragement in school, rejection in romance, defeat in business, friction at church, mistreatment in an estate settlement, disease, the death of a loved one may be influences generating bitterness. Multitudes encounter similar adversity and process it in healthy ways, but all do not have such resources. The weak eat grapes of wrath. They become men for one season, a winter of discontent.

The bitter, like Shimei, curse and cast stones as life's parade passes. After lengthy turmoil Job lamented, "Even today my complaint is rebellion . . ." (Job 23:2). 1 Samuel 1:10 describes Hannah as bitter because she could not have a child.

Some life-styles are programmed to cultivate bitter weeds. Peter denied his Lord, and for it he wept bitterly (Luke 22:62). Proverbs 5:3-4 teaches:

For the lips of an adulteress drip honey,
And smoother than oil is her speech;
But in the end she is bitter as wormwood,
Sharp as a two-edged sword.

With a mushroom cloud on the horizon, the question of Abner to Joab is pertinent for us, "Shall the sword devour forever? Do you not know that it will be bitter in the end?" (2 Sam. 2:26).

Families may be bitter. A husband or wife may become bitter at the other. Some parents are bitter toward their children. They did not want their children in the first place, and they think the children unfairly intrude into their lives. Many of our emotional disorders are the fruit of children harboring bitterness toward parents. Numerous complexes describe bitterness that siblings have for each other. The catalyst for the bitterness may be outside the home, but the fallout contaminates those one really loves.

Think of the families or friendships in the Bible where bitter weeds soured the relationship. Cain killed Abel, and Cain was marked for life. Isaac and Ishmael and their mothers became involved in a tug of war. Jacob tricked his father and betrayed his brother Esau. Joseph was sold as a slave by his brothers. Jephthah made a foolish vow concerning his own daughter. Saul's madness festered over Jonathan's friendship with David. David's own sons waged civil war to succeed to the kingship. Job resented his friends. Hosea had to learn to forgive his wife Gomer. The prodigal son's elder brother "became angry, and was not willing to go in" when the father celebrated his younger son's return.

In the twentieth century, many are caught in cross fires between warring family members, because bitter weeds have soured the milk of life.

Bitterness prevails even in the household of faith. Corinthian Christians serve in many churches. Paul, Peter, and Apollos have their adherents. An ecumenical age also knows of ecclesiastical ego trips which promote personal empire building. Diotrephes is alive and well, and he still loves to have the pre-eminence. Atmospheres are cultivated which view a church family in terms of "them and us."

Acts 2:44 records of the first church, "And all those who had believed were together, and had all things in common." Such commonness is so uncommon that it scarcely exists today. In the hymn, "The Church's One Foundation," we sing:

> Elect from ev'ry nation, yet one o'er all the earth,
> Her charter of salvation, one Lord, one faith, one birth;
> One holy name she blesses, partakes one holy food,
> And to one hope she presses, with ev'ry grace endued.[4]

Such words constitute a noble vision, but in no manner do they describe many contemporary churches which, like a centipede, scarcely know in which direction to move.

In John 17:11 Jesus prayed that His church might "be one." In early confessions of faith the church was confessed to be "one, holy, catholic (universal), and apostolic." In Ephesians 4:3-6, Paul gives us the basis of unity. It is twofold. It is the result of diligence and doctrine. In Ephesians 4:3 Paul writes of Christians "being diligent to preserve the unity of the Spirit in the bond of peace." Peacemakers are needed even in church.

The unity magnified in Ephesians 4 is built on doctrine. There is one body, one Spirit, one hope, one Lord, one faith, one baptism, one God and Father of us all. Unity will prevail in a church when barriers are broken. Ephesians 2:14 instructs us, "For He Himself is our peace, who made both groups into one, and broke down the barrier of the dividing wall . . ." Galatians 3:28 assures us, "There is neither Jew nor Greek, there is neither slave nor free man, there is neither male nor female; for you are all one in Christ Jesus."

Bitterness against God Himself is not unknown. A part of the grief process is a feeling of anger. Pastors, teachers, and others who comfort the grieving should be aware that the sufferer could express anger even at God. Jonah became angry because God forgave the Ninevites, as well as the fact that God sent a worm to afflict his gourd plant. Naomi said to the people of Bethlehem, "Do not call me Naomi; Call me Mara, for the Almighty has dealt very bitterly with me" (Ruth 1:20).

If a church is to be family, members must live in honor preferring one

another. If we are to achieve real community, we must abolish some frag-
menting bitter spirits—and we must live with malice toward none.

Bitter weeds grow in the field of nations. Exodus 1:13-14 records,
"And the Egyptians compelled the sons of Israel to labor rigorously; and
they made their lives bitter with hard labor . . ." Spin your globe and look
at the international bitter weeds. In the United States we still have socio-
logical hangovers from our Civil War over a hundred years ago. We have
made considerable progress in race relations, but we still have miles to
go and promises to keep, even in church. We must slay our bitterness
rather than our brothers. Move to Mexico, and we find a steady flow of
illegal aliens crossing the Rio Grande River. Civil war rages in El Salva-
dor. The United States is financing the overthrow of the government in
Nicaragua. A dictoratorship prevails in Cuba and Chile.

Frequently in the news is the oppression of the apartheid government
in South Africa. Afghanistan is divided by civil war. Lebanon is frac-
tured by a multiplicity of factions. Where can more intense bitterness be
found than among the Palestinians? Sikhs and Hindus are at each other's
throats in India. Terrorists are well organized. Practitioners of genocide
are all over the world.

Billy Graham has reminded us that ours is the generation that produced DDT to kill bugs, 2-4-D to kill weeds, formula 1080 to kill rats,
and $E=MC^2$ to wipe out populations.[5] Before Samuel hacked King Agag
to pieces, Agag said to Samuel, "Surely the bitterness of death is past"
(1 Sam. 15:32). The bitterness of death was not past for the king of the
Amalekites, and it is not past for us. Through governments, through
other corporate structures (including the church), through education and
in personal example, we must strive for the day when men will beat their
swords into plowshares and their spears into pruninghooks, when "nation will not lift up sword against nation, / And never again will they
learn war" (Isa. 2:4).

Faith's Responses to Bitter Weeds

What do we do when we find bitter weeds in our fields? Sometimes we
must eat them. There will be Marahs on our routes where there will be

no alternative but to drink bitter water. Occasionally everyone will have ashes for breakfast. Today I weigh 215 pounds, and I have been in excellent health most of my life. I can remember, however, a time in my boyhood when my mother thought I was not eating enough. She carried me to a doctor who prescribed some medicine, the taste of which would motivate anyone to eat more. It must have been made out of concentrate of bitter weeds.

In Revelation 10:9, an angel instructed John to eat a little book which made his stomach bitter. In Gethsemane, Jesus prayed that a cup might pass from Him. Such was not God's will so Jesus willingly drank the cup, but its dregs were bitter. Job received the news that his ten children were all killed in one day. The exiles who were taken to Babylon were so saddened that they could not sing the songs of Zion, but they had no choice other than to face the bitter waters of Chebar. Biting bullets is not good for the digestive system, but occasionally Bullet Burgers are all there is on the menu.

We make a second response to bitter weeds. We learn from them. We poison them, dig them up, put the cows in another field, anything to keep them from being a steady diet. A wise man learns from his problems. Even a man who fails should be wiser because of his failure. Nicholas Bentley affirmed, "Learning history is easy; learning its lessons seems almost impossibly difficult."[6] Walt Whitman had this insight when he asked:

> Have you learned lessons only of those who admired you,
> And were tender with you, and stood aside for you?
>
> Have you not learned great lessons from those who brace
> themselves against you, and disputed the passage with you?[7]

In learning, we learn that God is with us. He really is Immanuel. He wants to lead us from bitter pastures to green pastures. All things are not good, but God is at work in all things for good. Genesis 39:21 records that the Lord was with Joseph in prison. He was with the friends of Daniel in the fiery furnace. He will walk with us in our valley of the shadow.

In learning, we learn the power of prayer. We pray with Jesus in Gethsemane. We pray with Jonah in the belly of the whale. We pray with Paul and Silas in jail. We pray with the martyrs at the hour of death. We pray with Adoniram Judson at the grave of his wife in Burma. We pray with Washington in the snow of Valley Forge. We pray as the Holy Spirit makes intercession for us with groanings that cannot be uttered.

We respond to bitter weeds by using our circumstances to the glory of God. In 1984 a new law was passed giving some relief to consumers who bought new cars that were "lemons." The new law was commonly called "lemonade." As much as grace and gumption will allow, we take the lemons of life and make lemonade out of them.

In the town square of Enterprise, Alabama, there is one of the strangest monuments in the world. It is a monument to an insect. It honors the Mexican boll weevil. The boll weevil first came to Coffee County in 1895. The annual yield of cotton there had been 35,000 bales, but the boll weevil cut that by forty percent. Desperately trying to survive, the farmers began to raise corn, peanuts, and potatoes. In 1919, the county's peanut crop was over a million bushels annually. In that year a fountain was built across from the courthouse square in Enterprise, and on it an inscription was placed which read:

> In profound appreciation
> of the Boll Weevil
> and what it has done
> as the herald of prosperity
> this monument was erected
> by the citizens of
> Enterprise, Coffee County, Alabama.[8]

The monument is literally a monument to misery. A time of adversity became a source of blessing. As was the experience of Manasseh and Ephraim, some of our blessings are cross-handed blessings.

R. C. Buckner taught, "Bury all your troubles and plant flowers over their graves."[9] Bunyan's *Pilgrim's Progress* was written in Bedford jail. *Paradise Lost* was written by blind John Milton. Beethoven wrote many

of his symphonies after he was deaf. George Matheson had been blind
for twenty years when he wrote:

> O Love that wilt not let me go,
> I rest my weary soul in thee;
> I give thee back the life I owe,
> That in thine ocean depths its flow
> May richer, fuller be.[10]

A response to bitter experiences is to sweeten ourselves. We cannot
control others. We can control only ourselves. Burdens can make us bitter or better. Some are victims, not victors. They never leave the grave
side. They have soured on life. In the spirit of the imprecatory psalms,
they call down wrath on their enemies. Their plea is, "Stop the world. I
want to get off."

Others become better, not bitter. They grow under the burden. Character is developed. They mount up with wings as eagles. They are more
than conquerors. Their spirits are effervescent. They brighten the corner
where they are.

Psalm 84 describes pilgrims en route to the temple who anticipate the
beauty of God's house and the joys of worshiping there. Psalm 84:6
describes their journey with the line: "Passing through the valley of
Baca, they make it a spring." The precise location of the valley of Baca is
not known. The word "Baca" is derived from a root which means "to
weep." Baca was a barren, waterless area through which the pilgrims
passed. As they traveled through, they made it a spring.

The children of God should always find springs, resources which en-
able them to pass through Baca. They see heights beyond the valley that
others do not see. They have a Guide through the valley who knows the
way. He *is* the Way. Saints find wells that others never see. God's pilgrims hear a still, small voice whispering, "This is the way; walk ye
in it."

On Wednesday afternoon, January 15, 1986, I was visiting members
of my church who were patients in Memorial Hospital, Lake Charles,
Louisiana. One of the patients was Mrs. Helen Daigle, an elderly mem-

ber of our church. She was a devout Christian, but she had been in poor
health for about fifteen years. Prior to my visit that day she had been in
the hospital for about a month in critical condition. While I was in the
room with her, her husband, Lufus, asked me if I would like to hear her
favorite song. I was not sure how he intended for me to hear it, but I
responded that I would. One of the most inspiring moments of my life
was standing there and hearing a feeble, seriously sick woman, lying flat
on her back, sing with a weak but distinct voice the first verse and chorus
of "How Great Thou Art."

Respond to bitter weeds by sweetening yourself. When Moses came to
Marah, he threw a tree into the waters to sweeten them. I grew up around
sawmills and loggers. I have seen skidders snake many trees to the load-
ing area to be hauled to the mill. As a young boy I worked in a sawmill. I
wish I knew what kind of tree Moses used. What kind of tree might we
use to sweeten our bitter waters?

Throw in the tree of forgiveness. Nothing cultivates more venom and
bile than the attitude of getting even, holding grudges, settling scores.
The score keeper is the loser. G. Campbell Morgan observed that there is
nothing the devil hates more than a man who can forgive.[11] If we are
unforgiving we cannot sincerely pray the Lord's Prayer. Few men have
had more enemies than Paul, yet his instruction is, "And be kind to one
another, tenderhearted, forgiving each other, just as God in Christ also
has forgiven you," (Eph. 4:32). Concerning the forgiveness of Christ,
Karl Barth said, "To me—let me say incidentally—this fact of 'forgiveness' is even more astonishing than the raising of Lazarus."[12]

Take the initiative in using the forgiveness tree. In your marriage, in
your church, in your politics, on your job, take the first step to achieve
reconciliation. William Cowper suggested:

> The humblest and the happiest pair
>   Will find the occasion to forbear;
> And something, every day they live
>   To pity, and perhaps forgive.[13]

Throw into bitter waters the forgetfulness tree. Some continue bitterness over incidents that are ancient history. The mental rehashing of them rekindles their fire. Perhaps we will not be able to wash bitter experiences completely out of our lives, but we can quit making idols of them.

Throw in the tree of fellowship. Loners become bitter. Those in fellowship can reach out and touch someone, and they can be touched, which is a resource for healing. Many people are lonely. Some never receive a phone call or letter and never have anyone ask about them. Some of our popular songs express our loneliness: "I'm Mr Blue," "Blue Bayou," "Only the Lonely," "I'm So Lonesome I Could Cry," "Going Where the Lonely Go."

Loneliness is not the same as aloneness. Each of us needs times when he can be alone. God does not want us to be lonely. The first thing that God described as "not good" was man being lonely (Gen. 2:18). God does not intend for life to be a sentence of solitary confinement. God intends for life to be a cooperative program.

Throw the tree of fruitfulness into bitter waters. By our fruitfulness the world knows that we are disciples. The godly man is like a tree that brings forth fruit in season. One of the fruits of a Spirit-filled life is joy. One of the notes in John Wesley's journal reads, "I met Peter Bohler again, who now amazed me more and more by the account he gave of the fruits of living faith—the holiness and happiness which he affirmed to attend it."[14] Bitter weeds produce crop failures. A life of service produces fruit for an abundant harvest. Go out and help someone, and several waters will be sweetened.

Throw the tree of faith into bitter waters. Faith does not make things easy or simple, but it does make them possible. Moses had faith. From the Nile to Nebo he expressed it. With the murmuring and the manna, he exercised it. There are degrees of faith. Some have little faith, and others have great faith. Alexander Maclaren said that Christianity has fallen into the hands of a church that does not half believe its own gospel.[15] We need a growing faith, a daring faith, a faith that risks, a tough faith to match a tough love.

Kill the bitter weeds and plant fragrant flowers whose sweet aroma will impress the world. Paul wrote (Eph. 4:31), "Let all bitterness, and wrath, and anger, and clamour, and slander be put away from you, along with all malice." After all that he had been through, Abraham Lincoln taught us to live with malice toward none. Our supreme example is the Man upon the cross. No invective. No vengeance. No imprecation. Only, "Father, forgive them . . ."

4

Plow to the End of the Row

The reason God made a bulldog like he did was so he could hold on and still breathe.[1]*—Bud Robinson*

Introduction

When I was a boy, most farmers did their plowing with mules. Farm work was done by M and M, manpower and mulepower. Plowing did not require an extensive vocabulary. All one needed to know was "get up," "Whoa," "haw," and "gee." Plowing did require a lot of perseverance. When the sun was hot and the ground was hard, one was easily tempted to quit in the middle of a row and go to the barn.

Life itself can be as stubborn as a mule. Life's sun can be withering, and the ground can be unfruitful. When the inclination comes to forget the whole thing, God's word is, "Plow to the end of the row." In Matthew 24:13, Jesus put it, "But the one who endures to the end, it is he who shall be saved." James 1:12 offers the encouragement, "Blessed is a man who perseveres under trial; for once he has been approved, he will receive the crown of life, which the Lord has promised to those who love Him."

A cardinal doctrine of my denomination has been the "perseverance of the saints." As recorded in the New Hampshire Confession of Faith (1833), it affirms:

We believe that such only are real believers as endure unto the end; that their persevering attachment to Christ is the grand mark which distinguishes them from mere professors; that a special Providence watches over their welfare; and that they are kept by the power of God through faith unto salvation.[2]

True believers are persevering plowers. They plow to the end of the row.

Resources for Perseverance

How can one plow to the end of the row? When the hot sun is wilting your clothes, when your back is weary, when the sweat is stinging your eyes, when you ponder the fact that at the end of the row is a pile of troubles, how can you keep on keeping on? What moral *stickum* can we apply to our hearts that will make us perseverers?

One thing we do is exercise determination. *Webster's New Collegiate Dictionary* defines determination as "the mental quality, habit, or power of deciding definitely and firmly." Grit your teeth. Set your chin. Bend your back. Pass a personal resolution. Those kind do some good!

I have had class mates who succeeded in getting a college education because they were determined to do so. It may have required five or six or even ten years instead of the normal four, but they garnered their diploma. It may have required night classes, summer school, postponing marriage, and denying themselves numerous material pleasures, but they paid the price.

I have known husbands and wives whose marriage succeeded nobly, because they were determined to make it succeed. They refused to let pettiness, littleness, dirt, debt, or the devil defeat them. They exercised the wisdom, the forgiveness, and the discipline to make their marriage beautiful.

Businessmen have built successful businesses with determination. Determination certainly has its limits. There is more to success than determination or its lack. A man, however, who starts early and stays late and does not spend Monday, Wednesday, and Friday on the golf course will find pay day more enjoyable.

Some Christians have a meaningful "quiet time," because they are determined to provide for it. There are busy mothers and daddys who give their children ample prime time, because there is no "Out-of-

Order" sign on their priorities. There are churches whose ministries are blessed, because the church family refuses to play Trivial Pursuit. With determination the congregation has remembered that the gates of hell cannot close on the church. In the Christian life the big "D" is determination. It is always too early to quit.

A second resourse in the priesthood of perseverers is patience. Our age has been called the "now generation." I wish we were the "now generation" for God, but much of our nowness is in other areas. We live in a day when many things can be provided "instantly." We have instant coffee, instant tea, instant soup, instant potatoes, instant grits, instant cereals, instant lemonade, and instant pudding. Ours is a world of repairs made while you wait, of Jiffy Markets, microwaves, and one-hour dry cleaning.

In this hurried, instant-oriented world, it is worth remembering that God does not provide everything instantly. Answers to prayer do not always come while we are on our coffee break. Bible knowledge is not attained overnight. Christian maturity is not achieved in a week, a month, or a year. Influence does not come with a handshake. Leadership is not acquired in six easy lessons. By their very nature, some virtues require time, and time requires patience.

On April 1, 1987, I began having problems with my back. The problem was with a disc in the area of the fifth lumbar vertebra. For a week I crawled around the house about like Nebuchadnezzar grazing in his field. For about five weeks I limped around the church displaying the posture of the Hunchback of Notre Dame. On May 21 of that year, I had surgery which was successful.

Prior to and following surgery, I was very anxious to be well. I was not a very patient patient—as far as I was concerned, my medicine could not work fast enough. The exercise and other therapy needed to work faster. My incision needed to heal more quickly. My strength needed to return at a faster pace. A spiritual virtue I need to acquire is patience.

In James 5:7, James commands each of us to "Be patient." The Greek verb is *makrothumesate*. It is a first aorist active imperative. The imperative mode means it is a command. Patience is a divine mandate. *Thayer's*

Greek Lexicon states that this word means to persevere, to endure. Another Greek word for "patience" is *hupomone* which also means steadfastness or endurance. This word is used in James 5:11. Neither of these words convey the idea of stoic, passive endurance. Patience, inherently, has a spirit that overcomes.

Galatians 5:22 teaches that a fruit of the Spirit-filled life is patience. Psalm 40 begins:

> I waited patiently for the Lord;
> And He inclined to me, and heard my cry.
> He brought me up out of the pit of destruction,
>   out of the miry clay;
> And He set my feet upon a rock making my
>   footsteps firm.

Hebrews 12:1-2 challenges us:

Therefore, since we have so great a cloud of witnesses surrounding us, let us also lay aside every encumbrance, and the sin which so easily entangles us, and let us run with endurance the race that is set before us, fixing our eyes on Jesus the author and perfecter of faith, who for the joy set before Him endured the cross, despising the shame, and has sat down at the right hand of the throne of God.

Patience is required in every area of life. It requires patience to grow up. There is no "One-Hour Maturizing" that takes in boys and turns out men. It takes patience to be an outstanding athlete. Practice, practice, practice is required to shoot a basketball, hit a baseball, or throw a football. Patience is required to get an education. When James Garfield was president of Hiram College in Ohio, he received a letter from a father asking if the course of study couldn't be shortened from four years. President Garfield replied that it could. He continued to say, "But it all depends on what you want to make of your son. When God wants to make an oak tree, he takes hundreds of years. But it only takes two months to make a squash."[3]

One of the amazing things about the amazing Christ is His amazing patience. With all He had to do, with all the pressure, all the crowds, all the conflicts, all the enemies, all the crosses, including His final cross, Jesus was patient.

It took tremendous patience for Jesus to put up with His disciples. Judas betrayed. Peter denied. Thomas doubted. Others did not understand.

It took a lot of patience for Jesus to put up with His nation. He came unto His own, and His own received Him not (see John 1:11).

It took patience to put up with His neighbors in Nazareth. Jesus was one more prophet that one generation would kill, and the next generation would erect a monument to Him.

It took patience for Jesus to put up with the religious leaders. Basically, the people who really killed Jesus were preachers and seminary professors.

It takes patience for Jesus to put up with you and me. What flimsy excuses we offer! What games we play! What manipulation even of God do we try! What false fronts we put up! What masks we wear!

Do not grow weary in well doing. Be patient!

A third and greatest resource in persevering is the cross. Keep your eyes on the cross. Jesus is the perfect perseverer. Jesus sets His face stedfastly to go to Jerusalem (Luke 9:51). From His seven "My hour" sayings (John 2:4; 7:30; 8:20; 12:23; 12:27; 13:1, and 17:1) we learn that He set the clock of His life for Calvary. In Gethsemane Jesus asked the Father if there could be any alternative to the ignominious death of the cross. The answer to His prayer was "no." Jesus' last word on the cross was, "It is finished." If ever a man finished what He started, it was Jesus. At Calvary the finish was finished.

Keeping our eyes on the cross can facilitate our understanding of where the end of the row really is. That is a point of considerable obscurity on many contemporary spiritual itineraries. Keeping our eyes on the cross can, further, give us the fortitude to bear our own crosses.

Bear your cross. Plow to the end of the row. Don't be a drop out. Dr. Dale Moody used to quote the tongue twister, "If you fizzle out before the finish there was a flaw in your faith from the first." Don't fizzle. Faith it. G. A. Studdert-Kennedy wrote some lines about a man who kept his eyes on Christ.

We shall build on!

We shall build on!

On through the cynic's scorning,

On through the coward's warning,

On through the cheat's suborning,

We shall build on!

Firm on the Rock of Ages,

City of saints and sages,

Laugh while the tempest rages,

We shall build on!

Christ, though my hands be bleeding,

Fierce though my flesh be pleading,

Still let me see Thee leading,

Let me build on!

Till through death's cruel dealing,

Brain wrecked and reason reeling,

I hear Love's trumpets pealing,

And I pass on.[4]

Persevere in Potent Particulars

Plow to the end of the row in all of life's experiences. Plow to the end of the row in *preparatory disciplines*. Young people, stay in school. Don't be a dropout. More and more training will be required for life in our technological society. Preachers, continue to study. A preacher who is through studying is through. Dr. Paul Sherer told about a preacher who explained to his teacher that his practice in sermon preparation was to write the first half of his sermon and leave the second half to God. His teacher responded, "Sir, I congratulate you indeed! Your half is unfailingly better than God's!"[5] Engineers, doctors, lawyers, and many others must stay up to date, or they will be obsolete in a short period of time.

The future does belong to those who prepare for it. In our technological society, preparation is more important than ever. We Christians need to gird up our loins. The row we plow is God's row.

Plow to the end of the row in *dreaming*. Each of us needs a dream. Physically, all of us do dream, but apart from our sleep, we need to have a dream, an ideal of what God can do through us. Paint your life around your dreams.

In his book, *As A Man Thinketh*, James Allen said, "The dreamers are the saviours of the world."[6] Norman Cousins, editor of the *Saturday Review,* said, "What holds men back today is not the pressure of realities, but the absence of dreams."[7] We need to dream some impossible dreams that, by the grace of God, become possible.

Many things can threaten dreams. Poverty, sickness, unusually heavy responsibilities, early marriage, required military duty are among realities that can postpone the realization of a dream. Plow to the end of the row with your dream.

Plow to the end of the row in *Bible study*. On the Friday before he died, Dr. A. T. Robertson told his senior Greek class:

> I have been studying, preaching, teaching, and writing about the New Testament for over fifty years. But I never open my Greek New Testament without finding something I have never seen before.[8]

One never becomes smart enough, mature enough, or old enough to retire from Bible study. Bible study is not something that can be left to the young folks. If one is going to plow to the end of the row, he needs a sharp plow. The Word of God is sharp. In the second century there was a heretic named Marcion who chose his own canon. He rejected the entire Old Testament and limited the New Testament to Luke and ten of Paul's letters. Most of us are not so blatant as to go through the Bible with scissors in hand. We do mental editing. Mark Twain was right when he observed that the parts of the Bible that cause us the most trouble are those we understand, not those we do not understand![9] Even on the parts we do not understand, let us plow to the end of the row.

Plow to the end of the row in *prayer*. Prayer is serious, agonizing work. Prayer is far more than minutes of mumbling before going to sleep. Prayer is more than going through verbal motions. Our instant-oriented world produces patienceless pray-ers who do not understand the importance of prayer, providence, or perseverance. The answer to *maranatha* will take an eon. Other answers to prayer will require only centuries. To say the least, praying to the end of the row will require a lifetime.

Plow to the end of the row in *witnessing*. Ray Shawa, a deacon in the First Baptist Church of Lake Charles, Louisiana, tells of accepting Christ because Tubby Lyons, a deacon in the same church, witnessed to him at least once a week for two years.

When I was pastor of a mission in Louisville, Kentucky, I met a man who worked in a store in Florida. He had come to Louisville for one main reason: to witness to a friend. In Arizona a man attended our church who was thinking seriously about going to Pakistan to witness to a friend. People have accepted Christ at a funeral. Sometimes it is literally at the end of the row that the fruit is borne. In Burma, Adoniram Judson witnessed for seven years before anyone accepted Christ. Four years had passed before anyone even inquired about what it meant to be a Christian. I would have become a manic depressive seeing such meager results. Lesslie Newbigin said that the church needs to see itself going to the ends of the earth to the end of time.[10]

Plow to the end of the row in *theologizing*. We are all theologians. We are theologians of two hills, Mars Hill (the marketplace) and the Master's Hill (Calvary). Every generation needs to do its own theology. Every individual needs to do his own theology. In being a theologian, one never reaches the end of the row. Karl Barth said, "There can be no completed work. All human achievements are no more than prolegomena: and this is especially the case in the field of theology."[11] The Puritan, William Ames, said, *"Theologia est scientia vivendo deo,"* theology is the science of living to God.[12] Theology must be lived. It is not a hothouse or ivory tower discipline. It must be distinctly Christian. In his book, *The Experiment Hope,* Jurgen Moltmann laments what he calls a "chameleon theology," a theology that adapts itself to the environment around it rather than being a change agent for society.[13]

Plow to the end of the row in *service*. A few years ago, our gas stations provided a new service. There would be gas pumps on one island where a customer could pump his own gas, check his own oil, and clean his own windshield. This is the self-service island. At another island, station attendants would pump the gas, clean the windshields, and check the oil. This is the full-service island.

Such an option is a parable of life. We often discuss things *from which* we are saved. We are saved from our sins. We are saved from ourselves. We are saved from hell. Not so often do we discuss things *for which* we are saved. If we neglect the positive side we are going to stop at a half-way house whose effect is a spiritual bypass surgery, for the greatest joys are bypassed.

We are saved for God. We are saved for the present and future. We are saved for others. In spite of this, many life-stations are self-service.

Worship can be self-serving. In his book, *The Status Seekers,* Vance Parkard wrote:

> For the majority of American Christians, however, going to church is the nice thing that proper people do on Sundays. It advertises their respectibility, gives them a warm feeling that they are behaving in a way their God-fearing ancestors would approve, and adds (they hope) a few cubits to their social stature by throwing them with a social group with which they wish to be identified.[14]

The point has been well made that man needs a God whom he can serve, not a God to serve him.

Love can be counterfeited into selfish currency. When some say "I love you," they really mean "I love myself, but I want to do it through you." True love must give. It is never exploitive or manipulative.

One's business can be totally an exercise in self-interest. A businessman can give no thought to betterment of a community through better schools, churches, hospitals, and playgrounds. His philosophy can be, "I don't want it all, just the piece next to mine."

The joy comes when we are among those who fuel their lives at the full-service island. Full service does not neglect the self, but it includes

others, and it includes God. Full service lives by the motto of John
Wesley:

> Do all the good you can,
> By all the means you can,
> In all the ways you can,
> In all the places you can,
> At all the times you can,
> To all the people you can,
> As long as ever you can.[15]

Full service work is demanding. Christians go the second mile. If anyone asks for their coats, they give their overcoats as well. They become
fools for Christ. Their prayer is:

> Hallowed by *Thy* name, not mine.
> *Thy* kingdom come, not mine.
> *Thy* will be done, not mine.

A servant's work is dirty. Servants sit with the lepers, the prisoners,
the poor. Like Ezekiel, they sit with the exiles seven days. Sometimes the
servants sit in silence because they are wounded healers. Their presence
and their silence, however, are therapeutic.

The soldiers who win spiritual wars are not the generals, not the
preachers, but fishermen, chemists, teachers, and truckers, saints in
overalls and aprons. They are plain folks slogging through the ditches of
life.

Full-service work is divine. We are about the King's business. Dag
Hammarskjold, former secretary-general of the United Nations, wrote,
"I am the vessel. The draught is God's. And God is the thirsty one."[16]
Through our lives God wants to hang out a sign reading: "God at work."

Are you a servant? Where do you serve? Whom do you serve? Are you
willing to wash feet, to wait on tables, to do slave work? Are we willing
to say with John Knox, "I thank my God that I have come in the thick of
the battle"?[17] Can we pray with Augustine?

Eternal God,
the light of the minds that know you,
the life of the souls that love you,
the strength of the wills that serve you;
help us so to know you that we may truly love you,
so to love you that we may fully serve you,
whom to serve is perfect freedom.[18]

Plow to the end of the row in *living*. I heard Bishop Arthur Moore, the renowned Methodist preacher-bishop, tell of a little boy who wrote to his pastor, "Preacher, I hope you live all your life." Don't exist or just get by. Live! Oliver Wendell Holmes mused, "Many people die with their music still in them."[19] It was said of the race horse, Man O' War, "Some horses led him at the first turn, some led him at the backstretch, a few led him at the far turn, but no horse ever led him in the homestretch."[20] Stay out front in the home stretch of life. Michelangelo painted "The Last Judgment" when he was sixty-six. Alfred Lord Tennyson wrote "Crossing the Bar" when he was eighty. William Gladstone was elected prime minister of Great Britain, for the fourth time, at eighty-three. John Wesley was still a powerful preacher at eighty-eight.

Let us plow to the end of the row *as a nation*. To hear some preachers talk, America has one foot in the grave and the other foot on a banana peel. I don't believe it. Play no requiem for America.

America has not joined the "over-the-hill" gang. In the spirit of Mark Twain, the account of America's death has been severely exaggerated. To be sure, our nation has serious problems. We must mobilize our best minds and energies to address them. To hide our heads in the sand is to invite disaster. I think, however, that our past leaders have confronted problems and done many things right, or we would not be the greatest nation on earth. I think further that our mightiest victories are before us. There are more good people, more fine young people, more Christian people, more churches, more worthy institutions than there have ever been in America.

During World War II, Franklin D. Roosevelt wrote a letter to Winston Churchill in which he quoted some poetry from Longfellow. Roosevelt applied the lines to Britain, but they could be applied to America.

> Sail on, O ship of State!
> Sail on, O Union, strong and great!
> Humanity with all its fears,
> With all the hopes of future years,
> Is hanging breathless on thy fate![21]

Let each local congregation plow to the end of the row as a *church*. Let our influence be like leaven in the moral climate of our communities. Let our witness be a lighthouse to the lost and storm tossed. Let our resources be an encouragement to the struggling.

In Revelation 2-3, there are seven letters from the Lord to His churches. In every letter there occurs the phrase "to him who overcomes." Churches must overcome hardship, disappointment, discouragement. God's word to us is, "Therefore, my beloved brethren, be steadfast, immovable, always abounding in the work of the Lord, knowing that your toil is not in vain in the Lord" (1 Cor. 15:58).

Plow to the end of the row as an *individual*. When the sun is hot, the mule is tired, and the ground is hard, keep plowing. For forty years Frank L. Stanton was a columnist for the *Atlanta Constitution*. He was also poet laureate of Georgia. One of his poems is entitled "Keep A-goin'."

> If you strike a thorn or rose
> Keep a-goin'!
> If it hails or if it snows,
> Keep a-goin'!
> Taint no use to sit an' whine,
> When the fish ain't on yer line
> Bait yer hook an' keep a-tryin'—
> Keep a-goin'!
> When you tumble from the top,
> Keep a-goin'!
> S'pose you're out o' every dime,'
> Bein' so ain't any crime;
> Tell the world you're feelin' prime—
> Keep a-goin'!

> Drain the sweetness from the cup,
> Keep a-goin'!
> See the wild birds on the wing
> Hear the bells that sweetly ring,
> When you feel like sighin' sing—
> Keep a-goin'![22]

William Carey wrote to his nephew:

Eustace, if after my removal anyone should think it worth his while to write my life, I will give you a criterion by which you may judge of its correctness. If he gives me credit for being a plodder he will describe me justly. Anything beyond this will be too much. I can plod. I can persevere in any definite pursuit. To this I owe everything.[23]

I challenge you to plod, P-L-O-D. Keep a-goin'. Sail on. Keep dreaming. Live all your life!

5

The Hound of Heaven

Men are in flight all the day long. All of us flee continually: in silence or in gossip; in inertia or in boredom; in the pleasures of the table or those of the library; in the reading of a newpaper or in a piece of knitting; in sports or by the fireside; in witty sayings or idle discussions . . .[1]*—Paul Tournier*

Introduction

When I was a boy most farmers had several dogs. For some of my aunts, cooking dog bread was as common as cooking for the family. To this day most farmers probably have dogs. Lamar Catlett was a friend of mine who lived just up the Old Wire Road from my grandfather McDonald. Lamar had a collie that was the best squirrel dog I have ever seen. Lamar and I spent some pleasant mornings squirrel hunting as we climbed the gulleys of Alamucha Community.

In my younger days fox hunting was all the rage. Two of my uncles, Johnny Matthews and Sam Rollings, had several fox dogs, and when I visited them in the summer, they would "let" me go fox hunting with them. They made coffee that was thirty weight. They would drink their strong coffee and listen to the dogs run. Either of them could hear a dog bark a mile away and tell exactly which dog barked. From the sound of the dogs' barks, they could tell how close the dogs were to the fox.

Some in our community had coon hounds. I asked a man who worked on my grandfather's farm why he didn't go fox hunting. He answered, "I don't hunt anything you can't eat."

Some hounds were "soup" hounds. They didn't hunt anything but the food trough.

The Seeking God

Francis Thompson, an English Catholic poet, described God as a hound who pursues man. In his poem, "The Hound of Heaven," he wrote:

> I fled Him, down the nights and down the days;
>   I fled Him, down the arches of the years;
> I fled Him, down the labyrinthine ways
>   Of my own mind, and in the mist of tears
> I hid from Him, and under running laughter.
>   Up vistaed hopes, I sped;
>   And shot, precipitated,
> Adown Titanic glooms of chasmed fears,
>   From those strong Feet that followed, followed
>   after
>   But with unhurrying chase,
>   And unperturbed pace,
>   Deliberate speed, majestic instancy,
>   They beat—and a Voice beat
>   More instant than the Feet—
> "All things betray thee, who betrayest Me."[2]

As the hound of heaven, God knows man's scent. It is not Chanel #5. It is My Sin #1. Man has stunk up the place. During the past year a tug boat pulled a barge loaded with garbage down the East coast of the United States, and possibilities for dumping it were explored in areas along the Gulf coast. Finally it was pulled back to the northeast.

That is man's problem. He doesn't know what to do with his moral garbage. Worse, he scarcely recognizes it as garbage. In his book *Whatever Became of Sin?* Dr. Karl Menninger wrote, "In all of the laments and reproaches made by our seers and prophets, one misses any mention of 'sin,' a word which used to be a veritable watchword of prophets."[3] Organization man has exorcized the word "sin" from his vocabulary. Sin is more than "a psychopathic aspect of adolescent mentality." It is rebellion against God. It breaks not only God's law but God's heart as well.

In recent months commercials have appeared on television in my area which feature two "professional dummies." The commercial is shown to encourage the use of seat belts in cars. The two professional dummies have the appearance of robots. They walk in a disjointed fashion. When their car crashes, springs pop out of their heads.

There are plenty of professional dummies who are not television stars. The fact of a man refusing to deal with his sin problem certifies him as a dummy. At the age of accountability he turns pro. When it comes to sin, man is strictly major league. His proficiency is seen in a typographical error in a church bulletin in the listing of a hymn: "O For a Thousand Tongues to Sin." There was no typographical error in John H. Jowett's description, "And then there is the deadly, ubiquitous presence of human sin, in all its chameleon forms—well-dressed, ill dressed, blazing in passion, mincing in vanity, and freezing in moral indifference and unbelief."[4]

God knows our scent, and we are not hard to track. The increasing legalization of gambling, laws providing for abortion on demand, a high divorce rate, expressions of racial prejudice in which we slay our enemies rather than our enmities, a steady stream of homeless people in our streets, the easy access to drugs, and the rampant desecration of the Lord's Day are signs of our escape route.

As the hound of heaven, God is relentless in His pursuit. We try every trick in the book to throw God off the track. We lead Him through every moral brier patch in our asphalt jungle. We double back. We become devious. We vote God "Man of the Year" and pay tribute to Him in assorted currencies. We rationalize our sins. We resort to the theological trimming of God down to our size. We change our addresses.

God keeps coming. Nothing deters Him. Not critics. Not Caesars. Not cultures. Not congresses. Not crosses. Our Lord is always *Christus Victor!* We publish His obituary and announce that God is dead, but we learn that the account of His death (I am not speaking of Calvary) is greatly exaggerated. We fly our flags at half-staff, but we learn that it is our faith (not our flags) that has been lowered.

God is never thrown off the trail. God looks in every corner: Eden,

Egypt, Exile, everywhere. God is a retriever. He wants to bring us back. He wants to be our *go'el,* our redeemer, our Heavenly kinsman who will emancipate us from spiritual slavery.

God looks carefully. On July 27, 1975, my wife, Mary Ruth, and I drove to Tylertown, Mississippi, to visit her mother who lived in a rural area near there. Mary Ruth's brother, William, lived next door to Mrs. Magee. When Mary Ruth and I drove up, William was about to leave to help a farmer friend who had lost his wallet. The friend was Dale Rayborn who had been plowing with his tractor. Somehow his wallet had worked out of his pocket and had been lost in the field. The wallet had several hundred dollars in it, so several friends had been called to help hunt for it.

When we arrived, Rayborn, his sons, Nolan and Clint, and a friend were already searching for the missing wallet. The field was large and freshly plowed. The hunt was carried out by a friend driving a tractor that pulled some kind of plow through the field while others walked behind the plow to watch for evidence of the wallet. Three tractors were driven. One was pulling a disc; another was pulling a chisel plow; and the third was pulling a rotary hoe. I walked behind one of the tractors looking for the wallet.

Even with the field being plowed again, the clods of dirt were still quite large. As I walked I could easily imagine the wallet being turned over with a pile of dirt and never seen. I was beginning to be discouraged in the hunt when the wallet was found. A disc had cut a small corner off the wallet in turning it over. There was rejoicing because the lost was found.

Jesus is a careful hunter. He understands straying sheep. He has innumerable tracking stations, and He tracks us.

As the hound of heaven, God runs close to His quarry. We may follow "afar off," but God stays close to His prey. He crowds us. We can hear Him breathing. We hear His whispers. When we are caught, there occurs a close encounter of a Godly kind.

Close, however, does not count except in horseshoes. A football team that is close to the goal has not scored. A man who is close to marriage has not committed matrimony. A student who is close to graduation has no diploma. A man who is close to salvation is not born again.

The Bible is replete with accounts of men and women who came close, but they missed the boat of life. The rich young ruler affirmed that he had kept all of the Ten Commandments, but the indication is that he turned his back on Jesus. Jesus said to a scribe, "You are not far from the kingdom of God" (Mark 12:34). He was close, but he was not there. King Agrippa said to Paul, "In a short time you will persuade me to become a Christian" (Acts 26:28). Multitudes in hell were "almost persuaded."

The Surrounding God

In describing God as the hound of heaven who knows our scent, we are expressing the message of Psalm 139:7-12.

> Where can I go from Thy Spirit?
> Or where can I flee from Thy presence?
> If I ascend to heaven, Thou art there;
> If I make my bed in Sheol behold, Thou art there.
> If I take the wings of the dawn,
> If I dwell in the remotest part of the sea,
> Even there Thy hand will lead me,
> And Thy right hand will lay hold of me.
> If I say, 'Surely the darkness will overwhelm me,
> And the light around me will be night,'
> Even the darkness is not dark to Thee,
> And the night is as bright as the day.
> Darkness and light are alike to Thee.

This entire psalm describes God as inescapable. Man is a besieged city. God has us surrounded.

God is inescapable because of His habitat. Heaven, the uttermost parts of the sea, light, or darkness can be God's dwelling place. He rides upon a cherub and makes the darkness His canopy (Ps. 18:10).

In his *Church Dogmatics*, Barth wrote of God:

Therefore nothing will escape Him: no aspect of the great game of creation; no moment of human life; no thinking thought; no word spoken; no secret or insignificant enterprise or deed or omission with all its interaction and effects; no suffering or joy; no sincerity or lie; no secret event in heaven or too well-known event on earth; no ray of sunlight; no note which has ever sounded; no colour which has ever been revealed, possibly in the darkness of oceanic depths where the eye of man has never perceived it . . . Everything will be present to Him exactly as it was or is or will be, in all its reality, in the whole temporal course of its activity, in its strength or weakness, in its majesty or meanness. He will not allow anything to perish, but will hold it in the hollow of His hand as He has always done, and does, and will do.[5]

God notes the sparrow's fall. A little boy was trying to learn the Lord's Prayer, and he misunderstood the word "hallowed." He began the prayer, "Our father who art in heaven how do you know my name?" We may wonder sometimes how God knows our name, but He knows.

God is inescapable because of His habitat. God is also inescapable because of His holy love. The two greatest words in the Bible with which to describe God are the words "holy" and "love." God knows our down-sitting and our uprising. God knows our thoughts (see Ps. 139:2). Still He loves us. God's love is spontaneous, sacrificial, self-giving, value creating. This kind of love was described by Walker L. Knight when he wrote:

> Love has a way with me.
> Love embraces my concerns,
> looks deeply into my needs,
> caresses my pain,
> hears my longings,
> soothes my over-concern,
> talks about my strengths,
> releases the perfume of my self-respect,
> builds my hope once again,
> and creates, within me,
> a throbbing, pulsating desire for life.

> Love has a way with me,
> and love's way births new joy.
> Love enables me to help myself.
> Love doesn't embarrass me,
> or force itself upon me,
> or strip me of my pride.
> Love lets me give as well as receive.[6]

God's love begats love. It generates something in us that will not let us run from responsibility. Our crosses may be heavy, the assignment may be difficult, the adversaries may be many, but, like Esther, we have come to the kingdom for such a time as this, and in the agony we find the ecstasy of reflecting Christ.

Father George Tyrrell once wrote to his friend, Baron Friederich Von Hugel, "What a relief if one could consciously and conscientiously wash one's hands of the whole concern! But then there is that strange man upon his cross who drives us back, again and again."[7]

When you and I are tempted to indulge in self-pity, that strange man upon His cross sends us back, again and again.

God is inescapable because of His habitat. He is inescapable because of His holy love. He is inescapable, further, because of His heart searching. Psalm 139 begins with the words, "O Lord, Thou hast searched me . . ." The psalm ends with the prayer, "Search me, O God, and know my heart . . ." (v. 23). Jeremiah 17:10 records:

> I the Lord search the heart,
> I test the mind,
> Even to give to each man according to his ways,
> According to the results of his deeds.

God has sworn out a search warrant for man, and He signed it with His blood.

Saul of Tarsus felt the searching hand of God. He felt His hand as he personally saw the wondrous works of Jesus or was confronted by eye-witness accounts of them. I imagine he felt God's hand as he persecuted those whose faith in eternal life was stronger than Saul's zeal to kill them. Saul felt that searching hand as he held some coats and consented to the death of a young deacon who died very much like the Master by praying, "Lord, do not hold this sin against them" (Acts 7:60). Saul felt the long arm of God on the Damascus Road as he fully confronted the Christ whom he had not ceased to persecute and who had not ceased to search for him. Saul felt His search until he came to cry, "Woe is me if I preach not the gospel."

Jonah found out about the searching God. Jonah decided to get away from it all. Jonah thought, *I'll take myself a Mediterranean cruise. I'll go to Tarshish, and then the voice of God won't worry me.* Jonah should have purchased a round-trip ticket, because while he was asleep in the ship, the God who slumbers not was at work. Jonah learned that God's love was the love that would not let him go. He learned it as others came into danger because of what he had done. He learned it as the storm clouds began to gather about his life. Jonah learned it as the icy waters of the Mediterranean startled him fully awake to the fact that from God there is no escape. Jonah learned about God's love as God reached out His hand to save him from those waters.

This searching God knows us better than we know ourselves. Jesus answered the question of Nicodemus before he could even ask it. The woman at Jacob's well went into Samaria and said, "Come, see a man, who told me all the things that I have done; this is not the Christ, is it?" (John 4:29). Jesus knew the real problem of the rich, young ruler, and He had insight into the rock-like character of Simon Peter.

In *The Book of Common Prayer* of the Episcopal Church, one prayer reads:

> Almighty God, unto whom all hearts are open,
> All desires known, and from whom no secrets
> Are hid; cleanse the thoughts of our hearts by
> the inspiration of thy Holy Spirit, that we
> may perfectly love thee; and worthily magnify
> thy holy name: through Christ our Lord. Amen.[8]

God is the Lord from whom there are no secrets.

When I was a student at the Southern Baptist Theological Seminary, I used to go with a group to the Hay Market area of Louisville on Saturday nights where we would have a street service. Rather frequently we had our service on the corner of Jefferson and Floyd Streets outside a bar. We would sing, pass out tracts, try to engage those we could in conversation about Christ, and one of us would preach. You have to make points quickly when you are street preaching. We concluded a service one Saturday night, and I was standing on one corner waiting for some friends across the street who were witnessing to two men. One of the men was obviously anxious to leave, and soon he came walking across the street. Thinking I was just a passerby, he walked up to me and said, "Boy, I thought I would never get away from that preacher!" I made a remark to the effect that he should not want to get away. He stared at me and exclaimed: "Good grief, you're one of them." At least on that night, he felt like a lion in a den of Daniels!

The Seeking Sinner

For God's search to mean what it should, there must be some mutual seeking. This is the problem. Many use every resource to escape from God and not to be found by Him. As I read Psalm 139, I do not pick up the impression that the psalmist wants to escape, but he certainly considers the possibility. Many today consider the possibility, and they work overtime to make the possibility a reality.

There is a children's game called "Hide and Seek." In the game, all but one person will hide in the house or somewhere in the yard. One person is the seeker. He closes his eyes and counts to fifty while the others hide. In many experiences of life people play "Hide and Seek," but their efforts become much, much more serious than a game. Many use their energy in running or hiding from reality or responsibility or even themselves or God. The countdown becomes a countdown to Armageddon.

Have you ever wanted to get away from it all? Have you ever wanted to close the door and never look back? Have you ever run, even from God? I suspect that everyone of us at some time has at least dreamed of that tropical island where all is sunshine and comfort with no responsibilities, no deadlines, no problems, and no burdens to bear. Who of us at some time has not run from God?

Jeremiah experienced the rather common urge to escape when he cried out (Jer. 9:2*a*):

> O that I had in the desert
> A wayfarers' lodging place;
> That I might leave my people,
> And go from them!

Jeremiah thought he was too young to preach. He wanted to be a poet, not a prophet.

In the Garden of Eden, Adam hid from God. Men have been hiding ever since. Many today are running from God—running with fast cars, fast company, fast, frantic, hectic living in the fast lane. In *The Parables of Peanuts,* an interesting dialogue occurred between Charlie Brown and Linus.

"What if everyone was like you?" Charlie Brown asked Linus. "What if everyone in the whole world suddenly decided to run away from his problems?"

Linus replied, "Well, at least we'd all be running in the same direction."[9]

Gabriel Marcel has described modern Western man as one who has repressed his ontological sense and has run away from the awareness of his own being.[10] One worker held so many jobs during the course of a year that it took two envelopes to hold his W-2 forms.

Some run from God by using our noisy world to drown out the voice of God. The noise of industry, the jets overhead, the television in the house, the roar of the crowd, the chatter of daily commerce, the non-stop conversation of some motormouth people are used as mufflers for the "still, small voice." Somehow, somewhere, however, that soft, penetrating, persistent voice is going to get through to us.

Men run from God through addiction to drugs. The number-one drug problem in America is alcohol. There are more alcoholics in America than there are victims of all other drugs combined. There are more alcoholics in America that there are unemployed. Over half of the tens of thousands of Americans who die on America's highways each year are victims of alcohol related accidents. Seventy-five percent of all homicide victims have been drinking. Some people who are concerned about the drug problem among our youth or anyone else should begin by removing their six-packs and cocktails from the house.

Men run from God in many ways, but the message of Psalm 139 is that God is inescapable. When the psalmist wrote Psalm 139, he was on a high peak of inspiration. This psalm is the overflow of a life lived in intimate fellowship with God. Dr. A. F. Kirkpatrick says of this psalm, "The consciousness of the intimate personal relation between God and man which is characteristic of the whole Psalter reaches its climax here."[11]

You and I need to track God. We train our noses for spiritual scents that will lead us to clefts of the rock where we can see His glory pass. In his poem, *John Brown's Body,* Stephen Benet put into the mouth of Abraham Lincoln some lines which compare us to human hounds who join the chase for God. Abraham Lincoln recalls a man he knew who kept a kennel full of hunting dogs. He had all kinds of dogs—young, old, smart, foolish. Occasionally he would sell some of the young dogs, but he had one dog he would never sell. The dog was old and half deaf. The dog was not much on looks or speed. When asked why he did not sell the old dog, the kennel owner gave the reason that the old dog was terrific on a cold scent. He explained that once the dog got the scent, "He don't let go until he knows he's dead."

The Submission to the Search

Psalm 139 mentions some obvious results of God and man tracking each other. One is praise. Verse 14 reads, "I will give thanks to Thee; for I am fearfully and wonderfully made." Being found by God, we should sing "O for a thousand tongues to sing my great redeemer's praise." The entire Bible is a book of praise. All of life should be praise. Our practice will be in proportion to our praise. If God would charge modern man with spiritual malpractice, the root cause of our problem would be *malpraise*. Dr. George Buttrick said, "*Praise* means a 'breaking out' in spontaneous sound."[12] As it is the nature of birds to sing, it should be man's nature to praise.

The French word for "praise" is *preiser* which means "to prize." When we praise God, we prize God. When we praise God, we "press toward the goal for the prize of the upward call of God in Christ Jesus." It has been well said that the doxology is a life to be lived as well as a song to be sung.

When the Lord surrounds us, and when we say, "Sir, I would see Jesus," the result must be praise. Dr. Horatius Bonar, the Presbyterian poet-preacher, wrote:

> Speak, lips of mine!
> And tell abroad
> The praise of my God.
> Speak, stammering
> tongue!
> In gladdest tone
> Make His high praises
> known.[13]

Another result of finding God is joy. In verse 17 the psalmist declares, "How precious also are Thy thoughts to me, O God!" *Webster's Dictionary* defines "joy" as "gladness, delight, or the expectation of good." Those qualities characterize our personalities when we find the Lord. The Hebrew language uses thirteen different words for "joy" or "rejoice." Four of the words mean shouting, singing, dancing, or clapping. Galatians 5:22 tells us that joy is one of the fruits of the Spirit-filled life. First Peter 1:8 describes Christians rejoicing with "joy inexpressible and full of glory."

There is not much joy in our world. Ours is a day of sad sacks and crepe hangers. There is not enough joy in church! I agree with Saint Teresa of Avila who prayed, "From silly devotions and sourfaced saints, good Lord deliver us."[14] Joy is far more than humor, but it is no sin to laugh. Joy is found supremely in Christ. It is a by-product of our walk with the Lord who had a sense of humor.

A result of our spiritual rendezvous with God is submission to the leading of God. Psalm 139 closes with the prayer, "And lead me in the everlasting way." God does lead. He is not standing still. The footprint of the obedient sheep really is found within the larger footprint of the shepherd. Too frequently, we respond to God with words from an old commercial, "Please, I want to do it myself."

The word "submit" comes from two Latin words, *sub* (under) and *mittere* (to send). To submit is to be sent under, to be sent under orders, to yield one's will. It means we become pliable clay in the hands of the master potter. It means, as Dr. John R. Sampey preached, that we should "give Christ all the keys."[15]

6

Lost in Familiar Territory

Introduction

As I described previously, my daddy's home place was a farm in the eastern part of Lauderdale County, Mississippi. The farm was rather remote. The nearest town, Kewanee, was several miles away. Kewanee consisted of two stores, a cotton gin, a post office, and several residences. The road to the Lacy farm was (and is) unpaved. It is literally at the end of the road. When you arrived at the Lacys, you had to get out and walk.

When I was a boy, I would visit my grandmother Lacy several times a year. I thought I knew the terrain in the woods fairly well. One day my friend Richard Smith and I went out to the farm to hunt squirrels. We got lost. I never would have thought I could get lost in those woods, but I did. We must have walked up and down all the old logging roads before we came to a road about a mile from where we wished we had been. We wasted plenty of time, and the purpose of our trip was thwarted. I had become lost in familiar territory. Let me stamp your passport for an excursion into the land of the lost.

Facets of Lostness

There are several facets of lostness. There is physical lostness. If this occurs in a life-threatening situation when resources are running out, physical lostness can be terrifying. There is emotional lostness. Among our "divers diseases" is one the Bible names hardness of heart. Its symptom is callouses on the soul. One becomes emotionally anesthetized through the narcotic of non-love.

A facet of lostness is political lostness. As I write these lines, two political leaders in countries touching the Caribbean basin are under indictment by the United States government for what amounts to drug running. A few governments can scarcely function because of powerful drug cartels. Afghanistan is divided by civil war. In some areas, Protestants and Catholics, Jews and Palestinians slay their enemies rather than their enmities. There have been reports that the government of a central African nation hindered the distribution of food to its own starving citizens because of political tensions. Liberation theologians cry out for a political Moses to lead their countries out of the wilderness of corruption and oppression to the promised land of political reform. Years ago Bernard Baruch made a point: "We need in politics men who have something to give, not men who have something to get."[1] Amen!

There shines the facet of theological lostness. Barth observed that the Word became flesh and then theologians turned Him back into words. Donald McKim has written, "Accordingly, with rare exceptions, the formative voices in American pulpits and theological seminaries—whether conservative or liberal—have nurtured generations of church members and theological students in cultivated ignorance."[2] Who are the truly great scholars among us? They are present, but their tribe is not large. If you are a member of a denomination that genuinely supports scholarship and research and encourages the pursuit of truth wherever it leads, do not pass "GO"; fall on your knees and thank God!

There are churchmen who have responsibility for the theological leadership of millions of Christians who give every indication that they have achieved a black belt in theology. They think the canon is something one shoots at his competitors. Much that is published in the name of theology constitutes a discovery of the Dead Seeing Scrolls.

Ours is the generation (not the first) which has announced that God is dead. The pallbearers have been many. An autopsy will reveal that this has been a case of brain death, not God's, but on the part of followers who, in the spirit of Johannes Kepler, should be thinking God's thoughts after Him.

Social lostness has its wilderness wanderers. Our fragmented world has suffered a "wholacaust." We have lost our wholeness and our holiness. We have reversed *e pluribus unum* to the fact of *ex uno plures* (out of one, many). Albert Camus recognized our Humpty Dumpty sociology when he wrote that the most fundamental issue of life is whether or not one should commit suicide.[3] Too many are like Lucy who said, "I love mankind; it is people I can't stand."[4]

The worst expression of lostness is spiritual lostness. If man can find his north star spiritually, all his other lostnesses will disappear. Who is lost spiritually? Everyone is lost who is not in Christ. When I was a boy in our church's mission organization, Mrs. Fred Whatley, my leader, taught me that all are lost without Christ. In Luke 13:3, Jesus said, "unless you repent, you will all likewise perish." Jesus said of Himself, "For the Son of Man has come to seek and to save that which was lost" (Luke 19:10). Like the asses of Kish, man is lost. A creeping universalism is the influence of false prophets. Jesus is *the* way, not a way. Anyone who has not claimed Christ can use the bumper sticker: "Don't follow me. I'm lost."

In the New Testament, not to be saved means to lose one's life (Mark 8:35; Matthew 10:39; 16:25; Luke 9:24, 17:33). To lose one's life means losing everything (Mark 8:36). The Greek word *(apollumi)* for "lose" (passive: to be lost) also means "destroy." Such lostness or destruction is present and future and eternal. A lost man is like:

> A man without a country
> A ship without a rudder
> A pilgrim without a shrine
> A wise man without a star to follow
> A student without a school

> A soldier without an army
> A man without a flag to follow and without music
>   by which to march.

A man who is lost is out of orbit. He is a misguided missile. He is like a mad architect running up and down the corridors of life trying to find a way out. He is in a maze from which there appears to be no escape.

How lost we are without Christ! A poet has described our predicament in writing:

> Tangled in nets
> Of our wild philosophy
> Caught in the backlash
> Of ideas ill cast,
> Heaving the lead
> Into unplumbed infinity,
> Baffled, we stand
> Beside the shore at last.
> Snagged barbs, snarled lines,
> Torn sails! What fishers we!
> O man of Galilee![5]

There are many symptoms of our lostness. Is not the despair, the boredom, and frustration that characterize so much of life indicative of the fact that many have never found the way? The attempts to cauterize our moral consciences are symptomatic of our lostness. People resort to alcohol and drugs in attempts to forget.

No amount of success in life minimizes the danger of being lost. In 2 Kings 5:1 it is written of Naaman the Syrian that he was a mighty man of valor, "but he was a leper." It could be said of others:

> He is a wealthy man, but he is lost.
> He is a powerful man, but he is lost.
> He is a talented man, but he is lost.
> He is a civic-minded man, but he is lost.
> He is an influential man, but he is lost.
> He is a successful man, but he is lost.

He is a loving husband and father, but he is lost.
He goes to church, but he is lost.

Men are lost in an affluent society. We have learned to hate our neighbor going 600 miles an hour as well as at six miles an hour. Man lives not only on wall-to-wall carpet but in wall-to-wall confusion. With what Helmut Thielicke calls his "Babylonian heart," man has registered at a Babylonian Hotel for a lost weekend, and he has found that all of life is lost. We must hear once again the question of Jesus, "What is a man profited if he gain the whole world and lose his own soul?"

Factors Contributing to Lostness

What factors contribute to lostness? In the physical sense it could be lack of familiarity with the terrain, failure to observe landmarks, or clouds veiling the sun or stars. What contributes to spiritual lostness? In Luke 15 we find several answers. In response to criticism for His eating with sinners and publicans, Jesus related three parables. He told the parable of the lost sheep (Luke 15:4-7), the lost coin (15:8-10), and the lost son (15:11-32). In each case that which was lost was lost for a particular reason.

The sheep became lost doing what comes naturally. It nibbled itself into lostness. It wandered through the hills with its head down, thinking of its stomach, until it looked up, and it was lost. All that anyone has to do to go to hell is nothing. Go with the flow. Follow the crowd. Drift. Nibble along. Never look up. Edmund Burke was right: "The only thing necessary for the triumph of evil is for good men to do nothing."[6] It sounds rather vague, but "nothingness" can become an active, aggressive expression by one who has no interest in the Shepherd. Vance Havner shared the delightful story about the woman who would say "ner nuthin" instead of "or anything." A certain speaker came to her church. He did not open his Bible. He neither read nor quoted any Scripture, and his sermon was void of biblical content.

The woman was not accustomed to such preaching, so she went to the preacher afterward and said, "Well, that sure was some sermon. Never heard one like that before. You didn't have no scripture, ner no text, ner no doctrine—'ner nuthin.'"[7] The lost are those who have no way, no answer, no Savior, "ner nuthin."

He who does nothing is lost. A poet has put it well:

> He made no mistakes, took no wrong road.
> He never fumbled the ball.
> He never went down 'neath the weight of a load—
> He simply did nothing at all.
>
> He lost no hard fight in defense of the right.
> Never bled with his back to the wall.
> He never fell faint in his climb to the light—
> He simply did nothing at all.
>
> So death came nigh, for life slipped by,
> And he feared for the Judgment Hall;
> When they asked him why, he said with a sigh,
> "I simply did nothing at all."
>
> Oh, God will pardon your blunder, my friend,
> Or regard with pity your fall;
> But the one big sell that surely means hell
> Is to simply do nothing at all.[8]

The coin was lost because careless hands dropped it. Stamped on every life are the words "Handle With Care." Some lives will never see heaven, because careless hands dropped them. The careless hands may have been those of a pastor whose hands were busy with secondary things. The carelessness could have been with the pastor's tongue if it did not speak about lostness.

The careless hands could be those of a Sunday School teacher. Teachers, souls are under your care! You have the keys of heaven and hell! Take care! Visit! Pray! Share! The careless hands could be those of mother or daddy. Parents who don't set a worthy example for their children are guilty of child abuse. We are supposedly in good hands with a certain insurance company, and children are in good hands when the hands are attached to loving arms of godly parents.

The prodigal son was lost, because he chose to be lost. He picked his destination, planned his itinerary, selected his friends, chose his course. God made man a chooser. We are free in our choosing, but we are not free to avoid choice. We must choose. There is no fence to ride, no neutral ground. To be undecided is to say "no." William Jennings Bryan expressed, "Destiny is not a matter of chance. It is a matter of choice."[9] Robert Browning had one of his characters say, "Life's business is just the terrible choice."[10]

There are some who minimize mankind's power to choose. Behavioral psychologists would reduce many of our actions to conditioned reflexes. Humans however, choose their reaction to whatever hand life deals them. In Deuteronomy 30:19, God spoke to Israel: "I call heaven and earth to witness against you today, that I have set before you life and death, the blessing and the curse. So choose life in order that you may live, you and your descendants." Edwin Markham put it, "Choices are the hinges of destiny."[11] Every day you and I are confronted by choices.

> Should I take this course?
> Should I cheat on this course?
> Should I date this girl?
> Should I marry this girl?
> Should I start this habit?
> Should I take this job?
> Should I join this club?
> Should I join this union?
> Should I join this church?
> Should I invest in this business?
> Should I vote Democratic or Republican?
> Should I tithe?
> Should I take a social drink?

Over and over we are confronted by choices. Man is a deciding being. In a sense, choices become the stuff of which life is made.

Other factors contribute to one's sense of alienation. One is the impersonal world in which we live. There is a prevailing tendency to treat a person as a number rather than a neighbor. When a baby is born he may be child number 1234. A resident has a house number such as 2442. He has a Social Security number such as 428-54-5408. If he is a driver he has a license number. He may have an employee identification number. If he joins the army, he is given a serial number such as 59037864. He has a phone number. Now we have an income tax number. It is no wonder that modern man feels like a statistic instead of a soul. His name seems inconsequential.

The Far Country of the Lost

Jesus reported that the prodigal son went to a far country (Luke 15:13). What kind of country is that? It is a country of waste, because he wasted his substance with riotous living (15:13). What a pity it is to waste anything! In spite of the pity, so many are wasters. Our generation has been called the most time-saving generation in history, but what are we doing with the time we save? During this past week, how much time have we spent in worship, Bible study, prayer, and witnessing? One has observed that the world is watching America, and America is watching television!

To an alarming extent, we are wasting our natural resources. Some think of America as a land where people are standing knee deep in garbage, shooting rockets to the moon. Some people waste money. Las Vegas could be a symbol of that waste. There are more taverns in America that there are churches. In cigarettes, money goes up in smoke, and the habit is cancer by the carton. Others waste their talents. They sing the songs of the world but not the songs of Zion. Some lives are wasted. The thief on the Cross wasted his life. In the moment of death, his soul was saved, but he had no time to serve a church, care for his wife, set a worthy example for his children, or witness to his friends. His life was wasted. Tom Hood confessed, "My forty years have been forty thieves; for they have stolen strength, hope, and many joys."[12]

Spiritually, the far country could be near at hand. As with my squirrel hunting, a person can be lost spiritually in familiar territory. What familiar territory? One area could be our country, the United States. We commonly speak of our country as a "Christian nation," but, in any thorough sense, this is not true. According to statistics compiled by the research people of my denomination, there were between 155 to 160 million lost people in the United States in 1980, which was 68.9 percent of the total population. It is estimated that there will be 172 million lost persons in the United States in 1990. In most cities of any size one can find churches. A person can turn on his radio or television at almost any hour and hear the gospel preached. Christian books fill book stores, yet multitudes are lost.

Familiar territory can be a home that is predominantly Christian. There are homes where a mother or daddy, or both, are devout Christians, and a child grows to adulthood and is lost. A genuine example is set, prayers are offered, numerous Bibles are available, Christian literature and music are easily accessible, yet one is lost. When Park Tucker was a chaplain at the Federal Penitentiary in Atlanta, Georgia, I heard him tell about a preacher's son who had never accepted Christ until he came to the Federal Penitentiary as a prisoner.

Familiar territory could be the church. I do not want to disturb anyone's faith, but any objective scrutiny of the membership roll of many churches will reveal that large numbers are undoubtedly lost. Dr. Earl Waldrup wrote concerning our denomination, "The annual loss of active members is greater than the number of men which American Armed Forces have killed in battle in all the wars of this century. One out of every two persons on our church rolls is lost to kingdom service through his church."[13] Too often when new members come, we scarcely explain the plan of salvation, much less affirm great expectations of New Testament Christianity.

Dr. Gaines Dobbins wrote:

> Traditionally, we have too often considered the objective of evangelism achieved when the individual made commitment to Christ and the church. Yet any thoughtful minister, no matter how evangelistic in spirit, is bound to be disappointed when he makes careful study of a typical church membership roll.[14]

The church roll is a fertile field for evangelism.

The Folly of the Lost

The folly of the lost is that they cannot see their lostness. For a while the prodigal son would have thought he was on top of the world. Daily, he would have studied his stocks, royalties, and dividends. He would have owned a Mercedes and a Rolls Royce. His entertainment would have been X-rated. Smoking a little grass or sniffing a bit of cocaine would not have bothered him, but he could not see his lostness.

Martin Boehm was a Pietist who was struggling with a call to preach when it occurred to him that his basic problem could be his own salvation. His testimony was:

> I felt and saw myself a poor sinner. I was LOST. My agony became great. I was ploughing in the field, and kneeled down at each end of the furrow, to pray. The word lost, lost *(velohren)* went every round with me. Midway in the field I could go no further but sank behind the plough, crying, "Lord, save, I am lost!" . . . In a moment a stream of joy was poured over me. I praised the Lord and left the field, and told my companion what joy I felt.[15]

John Bunyan was deeply moved upon hearing his grandfather tell about seeing a man and his wife hanged. While the prisoners had been standing on the scaffold, the woman had begun to scream, "O God, I'm lost, I'm lost, I'm lost—I am soon going to hell! Oh, Why have I lived such a life?"[16] Following his grandfather's story, John Bunyan dreamed about the woman's screams.

Charles IX, King of France, confessed, "What blood, what murders, what evil counsels have I followed; I am lost, I see it well."[17] If the lost are to be found, if their folly is to be turned to faith, if they are to return to the Father's house, they must see and confess their lostness. The poet-preacher John Donne wrote, "I have a grave sin . . . Where Lazarus has been for four days, I have been for forty years."[18]

A serious question to consider is this: what if the prodigal son had succeeded in the far country? What if he had doubled his money? Instead of being reduced to the pig pen, suppose he had moved into the penthouse? Would his lostness have been changed? Emphatically not!

Finding the Lost

In the parables of Luke 15, we see the seeking Savior. The Good Shepherd is not content with the ninety and nine. The parable of the lost sheep teaches the importance of *one*. The one could be you or I.

You and I must join Christ in His search. When we really become concerned, most of us do what we want to do. We exert the effort, pay the price, and do what has to be done. Our problem is that of concern. In Augustine's terminology, the problem is rooted in the will. We sometimes serve as if churches were flooded with workers and there remained eternity in which to do the job. John Kennedy said, "We face opportunities and adversaries that do not wait for annual addresses or fiscal years."[19] We need to use the only time we really have, which is now.

A young man in Scotland sought his pastor's counsel because his love for Christ was growing cold. The old pastor led him to his study window overlooking the crowded streets. He said to the young man, "Christ is yonder seeking the lost. Go and help Him seek them, and you will find Him very near to you and very dear to you."[20] A person who is involved in healing the hurts of the world will always be close to Christ.

Actually, the search should be mutual. This is the case with the parables in Luke 15. In the first two parables, the one having lost something searches. In the third parable, that which is lost searches. As God seeks us, we should seek Him. Isaiah 55:6 counseled, "Seek ye the Lord while he may be found, call ye upon Him while he is near." An anonymous hymn writer sang:

> I sought the Lord, and afterward I knew
> He moved my soul to seek Him, seeking me;
> It was not I that found, O Savior true;
> No, I was found of Thee.
> I find, I walk, I love, but O the whole
> Of love is but my answer, Lord, to Thee!
> For thou wert long beforehand with my soul;
> Always Thou lovedst me.[21]

At nine thirty in the evening, on Tuesday night, March 15, 1966, I received a telephone call from my friend Robert Earl Gordon who lived on Louise Street in Hapeville, Georgia. He informed me he had heard over the radio that the three-year-old son of a former deacon and Sunday School superintendent in our church was lost in the woods near his home. Robert Earl and I agreed to go down and help with the search. Before I could leave, Mrs. J. P. Ray called and also asked if I knew about the son being lost. She reported that her husband and C. C. Martin were also going to aid in the search, and I asked her to have them pick up Robert Earl and me. On the way we stopped by the Hapeville Police Station to see if we could borrow a few powerful flashlights. While we were there, Officers Hugh Brown, Melvin Denny, and Jack Grant volunteered to join in the search.

When we arrived at the deacon's home in Fayette County, we found that a large number of men for several hours had been searching the woods back of the house. Someone had waded a creek twice, and men had looked around the edge of an old pond. Over three hundred people joined in the search. Civil Defense Units were present. There were policemen and firemen from Fayetteville, College Park, Riverdale, Hapeville, and Forest Park.

The search was well organized. Men would line up in long lines and walk through the woods and fields. Finally, when some had begun to wonder if the son was lost in a pond or if he had been picked up by someone in a passing car, he was found about two o'clock in the morning, asleep in the woods. All of us were ecstatic upon finding him, and a prayer of thanksgiving was offered.

The Fellowship of the Found

When a lost person is found, he can sing with John Newton:

> Amazing grace! how sweet the sound
> That saved a wretch like me!
> I once was lost, but now am found,
> Was blind but now I see.[22]

With David, we can find the joy of our salvation. With Paul we can exclaim, "Rejoice in all things and again I say, rejoice." Christianity should be joyful. Like Saint Theresa, we can pray to be delivered from "frowning saints."

In Jesus' story we relate to the joy of finding the lost sheep. Jesus said, "I say unto you, that likewise joy shall be in heaven over one sinner that repenteth, more than over ninety and nine persons, which need no repentance" (Luke 15:7). The joy in heaven is in contrast to the grumbling of the Pharisees and Scribes. We may have many images of heaven, but one of them must include joy. Joy is the priority business of heaven. Leon Bloy said, "Joy is the infallible sign of the presence of God."[23] God being present in our lives, we should be joyful.

C. S. Lewis entitled the story of his conversion *Surprised by Joy*. Upon the conversion of one person, joy reverberates down the corridors of heaven. God the Father kills the fatted calf and throws a banquet. For the joy that was set before Him, Jesus endured the cross. Joy is set before Him when one of us stands at the foot of that cross. When Jesus was born, the angels sang "Glory to God in the highest . . ." When a sinner is born again, they sing the second verse. The twenty-four elders around the throne give a victory shout. There is dancing on the streets of gold when one person trusts Christ. The hills clap their hands, and the morning stars sing together!

7

Well Water

To find the water of life, one needs, not a divining rod, but a divine rod. —William J. Lacy

Introduction

When I was born my family did not have running water in the house. Our water came from a well. In my early years we moved from Mississippi to Alabama, and our house there did not have water piped to it. The source of our water was a well. A generation ago, many people in rural areas got their water from a well or a cistern. Drinking water was kept in a bucket that may have been located on the back porch or gallery. A dipper, sometimes made out of a gourd, would have been with it. Frequently, the barn and lot would have been located near the well, and a sluice would have led from the well to a trough in the lot. The cows and mules would have their water via buckets of well water being fed into the trough. The Saturday night bath would have been taken in a wash tub. One of my oldest memories is of going to the well with someone at our house and seeing a snake in the water bucket when it was drawn to the top of the well.

It may be nostalgia or a faulty memory, but it seems to me that no water has ever tasted so good as water from the wells where I grew up. I assure you that the Environmental Protection Agency would not have worried about it being contaminated. It was like the Lord had made it.

Wells are mentioned frequently in the Bible. Abraham dug wells. The Philistines filled some of them up, and they had to be re-dug. At a well in

Nahor the servant of Abraham met Rebekah with whom a marriage with Isaac was arranged (Gen. 24:10-27). At a well Moses met seven daughters of Reuel, the priest of Midian (Ex. 2:15-16). Moses would marry one of the daughters, Zipporah. In Numbers 21:17-18 is the song of the well. In Judges 1:15, Achsah requested of her father Caleb. "Give me a blessing, since you have given me the land of the Negeb, give me also springs of water." In Bible times a well frequently determined the location of a city.

One of the most beautiful stories in the Bible is the story of David, camped with his mighty men while his forces were in combat with the Philistines (2 Sam. 23:11-17). Probably as a casual remark David commented, "Oh that someone would give me water to drink from the well of Bethlehem which is by the gate!" Three of David's mighty men took him seriously. They slipped through the enemy lines, drew water from the well at Bethlehem, and brought some back to David. Recognizing their heroism, David was so moved he would not drink it, "but poured it out to the Lord" (2 Sam. 23:16).

In John 4, we read about Jesus' coming to a well. It was Jacob's well at Sychar, which is commonly identified with modern Askar. The well had been there over a thousand years when Jesus arrived there. It is still there today. I have drunk from Jacob's well. At the well Jesus met a woman. In the conversation between them, we read Jesus' message on the water of life. Jesus shared this message with only one person, the woman at the well.

Jesus was the busiest man who ever lived. Throughout much of His ministry, large crowds followed Him. They surrounded the homes where He stayed. On one occasion four men tore a hole in a roof to gain access to Him. On another occasion the crowd almost pushed Jesus into the Sea of Galilee. One crowd numbered over 5,000 men. More people needed to see Jesus than have ever needed to see any other man, and Jesus' work was more important than the work of any other person.

As busy as He was, Jesus always had time for the individual. There are at least nineteen times in the four Gospels when Jesus taught only one person. Whether it was speaking to a young child whom Jesus used as an object lesson or to Matthew, called from his place of customs, or to Nicodemus, the rabbi who came by night, or to the woman taken in adultery whom He instructed to go and sin no more, or to Zaccheus, a corrupt tax collector, or to the nobleman of Capernaum or to a critical lawyer or to the rich young ruler, clothed in the pious robes of his self righteousness, or to the woman at Jacob's well, Jesus was never too busy to share His profoundest truth with one person. Jesus recognized the power of one. We should appreciate the lines of Edward Everett Hale:

> I am only one,
> But still I am one,
> I cannot do everything,
> But still I can do something;
> And because I cannot do everything
> I will not refuse to do the something that I can do.[1]

Never underestimate one vote, one prayer, one witness, one influence.

Prophetic Water

Jesus had a one-on-one interview with the woman at Jacob's well. The story of this conversation with the woman is recorded only by John (chapter 4). Their dialogue is the most extensive and intensive that we have preserved from the ministry of Jesus. This particular passage is related to preceding chapters in two ways. (1) The common theme in chapters 2, 3, and 4 is that, in Jesus, Judaism and the Old Testament are fulfilled. This was the point in John 2:1-11 when the content of the pots for purification was changed to wine. (2) A second relationship is in the use of the term "water." Obviously, this was a subject in chapter 2 when the water was changed to wine. It entered the teaching of Jesus in John 3:5 when He said: "Truly, truly, I say to you, unless one is born of water and the Spirit, he cannot enter into the kingdom of God."

In John 4, water is also the primary subject. In John 7:37-38, Jesus said: ". . . If any man is thirsty, let him come to Me and drink. He who believes in Me, as the Scripture said, 'From his innermost being shall flow rivers of living water.'" The background to this statement by Jesus was the Feast of Succoth (Feast of Tabernacles). An important rite at this festival was the ceremony of the water-drawing. On each day of the Feast, priests took a golden pitcher to the Pool of Siloam in the Kidron Valley. They filled it with water and, accompanied by appropriate praises, carried it to the temple. There, at a designated time, the priest who was leading in worship poured the water into a silver container on the altar. This ceremony called to mind the mercy of God when water was provided in the desert.

Water is a common symbol throughout the Scriptures for God's saving activity. This is understandable since the early Hebrews were nomads. As they traveled with their flocks, water was a treasured necessity. It could easily be equated with life. The psalmist sang of God, "He leadeth me beside still waters." Isaiah 55:1 invited the world to drink of waters that satisfy man's most basic needs. God spoke to Israel through Jeremiah (2:13) with the indictment:

> For My people have committed two evils:
> They have forsaken Me,
> The fountain of living waters,
> To hew for themselves cisterns,
> Broken cisterns,
> That can hold no water.

Zechariah 14:8 contains the prophecy: "And it will come about in that day that living waters will flow out of Jerusalem, half of them toward the eastern sea and the other half toward the western sea; it will be in summer as well as in winter." Ezekiel 47:9 spoke of rivers of healing. Revelation 22:1 shares the vision, "And he showed me a river of the water of life, clear as crystal, coming from the throne of God and of the Lamb."

John 4 begins with a statement that Jesus knows the Pharisees have heard about the success of His ministry. Jesus also knew the Pharisees, and in Matthew 23:13-36, He severely rebuked them. Jesus knew the heart of Nicodemus, and He answered his question before Nicodemus could ask it. Jesus knew the character of Simon Peter was like a rock. He knew that Nathanael was without guile. He knew that the rich young ruler lacked one thing. What amazing insight Jesus had into the hearts of men and women! John 2:23-25 (KJV) describes the insight of Jesus with the words:

> Now when he was in Jerusalem at the passover, during the feast, many believed on his name, beholding his signs which he did. But Jesus did not trust himself unto them, for that he knew all men, and because he needed not that any one should bear witness concerning man; for he himself knew what was in man.

Psalm 139 describes the searching eye of God with the beautiful words:

> O Lord, Thou hast searched me and known me.
> Thou dost know when I sit down and when I rise up;
> Thou dost understand my thought from afar.
> Thou dost scrutinize my path and my lying down,
> And art intimately acquainted with all my ways (Ps. 139:1-3).

During the course of Jesus' conversation with the woman of Samaria, it became clear that He knew her heart. Without being told, Jesus mentioned the five husbands she had had (John 4:18). Later, she went into Samaria and said to the people, "Come, see a man, who told me all the things that I have done" (John 4:29).

If Jesus knew the woman of Samaria and Nicodemus so well, He knows the hunger of our hearts, the emptiness and frustration we experience, the lust and envy that we desperately wish did not exist. Things that mother and daddy, husband and wife do not know, God knows. Things that no one else on earth knows, God knows. A little boy wrote a letter to the Lord:

> Dear God,
>   If you know so much how come you never made the river big enough for all the water and our house got flooded and now we got to move?—Victor[2]

The Lord may not divert the floods, but He does know so much. The wonder of wonders is that He continues to love us.

Because Jesus knew the Pharisees's envy and animosity, Jesus decided to leave Judea. Each time thereafter that Jesus returned to Judea there was an open disagreement with the Pharisees who attacked Him (John 5:1-47; 7:14-10:21; 10:22-42; 11:17-53). On His last visit to Jerusalem, the Pharisees succeeded in putting Him to death.

Polluted Water

As Jesus left Judea, John 4:4 records: "And He had to pass through Samaria." In Luke 2:49, Jesus said He had to be in His Father's house. In Mark 8:31, He taught that He *must* go to Jerusalem and suffer. Some things were not optional in Jesus' life. Some things were divine imperatives. The love of God constrained Him to certain ministries.

There should be some essentials in every life. I pray there are some things in each of our lives toward which we refuse to have a "take-it-or-leave-it" attitude. Worship should provide spiritual food without which we cannot live. Is the Bible an unread best-seller or a road map for our souls? Is prayer something nice to talk about or a resource that strong souls must draw upon? Is the church a building on some street or the body of Christ, the bride of Christ, the temple of the Holy Spirit? Are there priorities in our lives? Can we say with the psalmist, "As the deer pants after the water brooks,/ so my soul pants for Thee O God"? (Ps. 42:1).

One thing that Jesus had to do was pass through Samaria. Jesus was leaving Judea and going to Galilee. Samaria lay between the two, but in the first century strict Jews took the long road. They crossed the Jordan and traveled through Perea. Then they recrossed the Jordan to enter Galilee. Back of this itinerary, involving going out of the way, lay centuries of animosity and tensions between strict Jews and the Samaritans who regarded themselves as Jews. The tensions had produced the "Samaritan schism."

Samaria was the name given by King Omri to his new capital city (1 Kings 16:24). The Samaritan religious sect originated with a romance in the family of the Jewish high priest. One of his sons married a foreign wife, the daughter of Sanballat the Horonite (Neh. 13:28). Nehemiah and Ezra commanded that marriages with foreigners were to be annulled and that the foreign wives and their children should be driven out. The son of the high priest refused to disown his wife so he was driven out of his community. His father-in-law, Sanballat, built him a temple on Mount Gerizim. Mount Gerizim was chosen because it is the only site mentioned by name in the Law for the worship of God after the conquest (Deut. 11:29; 27:4-8,11-14).

The religious leaders at the Mount Gerizim temple started what came to be the Samaritan sect. Before and after the particular incident that led to the building of the Mount Gerizim temple, things happened that alienated the peoples of the Samaritan and Judean regions. In 931 BC, following the death of Solomon, the kingdom of Israel was divided with the tribes of Judah and Benjamin constituting the southern area. In 722 BC, Samaria and the Northern Kingdom fell to the Assyrian armies. The Assyrians brought many of their own people to live in the area (2 Kings 17:24f.), and this led to suspicions of tainted religious practices. After the return from the Babylonian exile, Nehemiah refused the offered help of Sanballat. In 107 BC, John Hyrcanus, the priest-king of Judea, captured Samaria and destroyed the temple on Mount Gerizim. He tried to force the Samaritans to conform to Jerusalem's version of orthodoxy, but he was unsuccessful. When the Romans came, the Samaritans were freed from Jewish rule.

There still exists a small group of Samaritans consisting of less than 500 people. An important text for the study of the Old Testament is the *Samaritan Pentateuch*.

Because of tensions built up over a thousand years, during Jesus' earthly ministry, the Samaritans were looked upon by strict Jews as second-class citizens. John 4:9 records, "For Jews have no dealings with Samaritans." When one group will have no dealings with another group, the water of relationships is polluted.

In the light of social attitudes, it is distinctly noteworthy that Jesus felt He *must* go through Samaria. In this context, it is important to mark other statements about Samaritans in the New Testament. One of Jesus' most unforgettable parables was about a Samaritan (Luke 10:25f.) who befriended a man whom a priest and a Levite had neglected. When Jesus healed ten lepers (Luke 17:11-19), only one of them paused to say "thank you." The one was a Samaritan (Luke 17:16). In Luke 9:51-56, the disciples were trying to find a place for Jesus to lodge during His journey. A Samaritan city refused Jesus its hospitality.

James and John asked, "Lord, do You want us to command fire to come down from heaven and consume them?" Jesus rebuked them for asking such a question.

In the missionary commission of Acts 1:8, the church was challenged to win Samaria. In Acts 8, one of the earliest missionary efforts of the church was to Samaria. What does this say to us? It says that when New Testament Christians answered the question "Who is my neighbor?" they included the most desperate, the poorest, the most illiterate, the most disenfranchised outcasts who constituted the dregs of society. Somewhere along the line, probably quite early, the church lost this spirit. The church polluted the pure water of love. We dismissed the "keeper of the spring," and the church has had a terribly challenging time exemplifying incarnational love.

In going through Samaria, Jesus crossed some boundaries of class. It was not normal for a rabbi to have an in-depth conversation with a woman. In 150 BC, Rabbi Jose ben Johanan of Jerusalem taught that men should not talk about serious matters with women. Some rabbis taught, "It would be better to see the Torah burnt than to hear its words upon the lips of women."[3] In the course of time, Jewish men prayed every day, "Blessed art Thou, O Lord our God, who hast not made me a woman."[4] In Bible times, a woman had no rights of inheritance if there were male heirs (Num. 27:1-11). According to Deuteronomy 24:1-4, a man could divorce a woman, but a woman could not divorce a man. Women could not enter the main sanctuary of the temple, and women could not participate in the offering of sacrifices.

Jesus treated the woman at the well as if He thought she was important. He regarded her as somebody. His example and teachings have had a liberating influence that has helped free women from shackles of mistreatment and servitude. The twentieth-century church needs to give full recognition to the dedication and talents of women and let them participate in the leadership of the church through opportunities provided on a level playing field. A misogynous, androcentric church is not going to fulfill a servant model for the body of Christ.

In going through Samaria, Jesus crossed some boundaries of prejudice. Prejudice is one of the main pollutants which contribute to a malignant spirit. There are many types of prejudices. There are political prejudices. I have known people who would not vote for a certain party if the Lord were on the ticket. There are national prejudices. It was spoken of Alexander Pope that he mistook a group of English gentlemen for all mankind.[5] There are religious prejudices. Bertrand Russell quipped, "A great majority of the human race has religious opinions different from our own, and therefore groundless."[6] It is not hard to find a church arrogant enough or ignorant enough to think it has the market cornered on the truth.

There is racial prejudice. The late Rabbi Julian Feibelman of Temple Sinai in New Orleans said, "The Pilgrim fathers landed on their knees and then they landed on the Aborigines."[7] The dictionary tells us that prejudice is an opinion formed without knowledge, thought, or reason. Voltaire said prejudice is "the reason of fools."[8] Jesus had no second-class citizens or any second string. His gospel and His love were for all men. What He did for any man He would do for every man, even the Samaritans. Our love can do no less. The invitation of our hearts and churches must be "whosoever will." Any church that refuses a person because of the color of his skin should write "Ichabod" across its entrance, because the glory has departed.

Jonah was a prejudiced preacher. He thought the Ninevites lived on the wrong side of the tracks. It was acceptable to him if God gave them forty days and "nuked" them. Even under divine duress, Jonah was not letting them in his church. Jonah bought a ticket to Tarshish, and he "paid the fare thereof." The price of prejudice is always high. Too high!

The price of prejudice is the loss of self-respect. Lack of respect for others is a symptom of the lack of respect for self. It is further a symptom of a lack of respect for God. One's attitude toward other races is a barometer of one's attitude toward God. The accusation for which Jesus was

102 BITTER WEEDS AND BURNING BUSHES

tried was nailed to the cross in three languages, Hebrew, Greek, and Latin. This means that Jesus died for every person. Every person is made in the image of God. As the pennant-winning Pittsburg Pirates emphasized a few years ago, "We are family."

The price of prejudice is disobedience. The Lord commands us to love and to bear one another's burdens. When we exploit and manipulate, we follow the footprints of every racist from Haman to Hitler. The final solution to our racial final solutions is loving obedience. On every person's map, there are only two spiritual destinations, Nineveh and Tarshish. The Tarshish trip bypasses obedience.

The price of prejudice is a polluted heart. As Lincoln admonished, we should live with "malice toward none." If we do not, our hearts will shrivel until they resemble prunes. The pure of heart not only see God, they also see their brothers. At the house of Cornelius, Peter had a vision enabling him to enlarge the circle of his concern to include the Gentiles. Many in the family of God need to enlarge their circles of concern. Thoreau was wise in saying, "It is never too late to give up our prejudices."[9]

Personal Water

Jesus talked with the Samaritan woman. Jesus initiated and ended the conversation. He opened the conversation by asking her for a drink of water. Jesus began where people were. We do not teach calculus to first graders, and we do not begin a new-member orientation by explaining the Trinity. We must begin where people are. Jesus used very familiar themes such as bread, light, leaven, sowing seed, sheep, and, with the woman at the well, water.

John 4 is a chapter of contrasts. There is a contrast between the water of the well and the water which Jesus gives. There is also a contrast between Jacob and Jesus as givers of water. Jesus observes that those who drink the water of the well will thirst again (John 4:13). Those who drink the water that Jesus offers will never thirst again (John 4:14). The water of life is actually Christ Himself. It is personal water. Jesus came to meet our most basic needs. If only we would let Him! So much of our energies are involved in activities that may keep us busy, provide some meaning and offer some pleasure, but we thirst again. Their satisfaction is short-lived.

Many people do not find their basic needs met because they have tried to impeach God. They have removed Him from their thinking and refused to recognize Him as Lord. It has been observed that man's greatest need is to know what is his greatest need. Our greatest need is for God. Pascal wrote, "There is a God-shaped vacuum in the heart of every man which cannot be satisfied by any created thing, but only by God."[10] Augustine confessed, "Thou hast made us for thyself, O God, and our souls are restless until they find their rest in thee."[11] Samuel Logan Brengle said of Jesus:

> Christ is my meat, Christ is my drink,
> My medicine and my health;
> My peace, my strength, my joy, my crown,
> My glory and my wealth.
>
> Christ is my Father and my Friend,
> My Brother and my Love;
> My Bread, my Hope, my Counselor,
> My advocate above.
>
> My Christ, he is the Heaven of heavens,
> My Christ, what shall I call?
> My Christ is first, my Christ is all,
> My Christ is All-in-All![12]

As Jesus talked with the woman at the well, she became evasive. When He mentioned her husband, her response was that she had no husband (John 4:17). In John 4:20, she raised a controversial subject concerning the proper place of worship, Mt. Gerizim or Jerusalem. So often people who need God become evasive. They don't want to get serious. Many people make attempts to sidetrack the witness. They raise points about baptism or where Cain got his wife, anything but an awful moment of truth. Too many have been playing church. They attend. They have sung the hymns and heard the prayers, but they do not intend to get down to cases about God. People should take off the masks, quit playing church, and become transformed and transforming Christians.

That is what the woman at the well did. She had gone through five husbands. Can you imagine the heartache she had been through? She had been used and exploited. She may have given up on happiness until one day at a well, all things became new. She rushed into town and began to tell people about Jesus (John 4:29). The Gospel of John has much to say about witnesses to Jesus. John the Baptist is a witness (1:6-7). God the Father is a witness (5:37; 8:18) as is Jesus Himself (8:14,18). The Old Testament points to Jesus (5:39,46), and the works of Jesus indicate who He is (5:36; 10:25; 14:11). Those who saw His works testify (4:39; 9:25,38; 12:17). His disciples become witnesses (15:27; 21:24). An important part of the ministry of the Holy Spirit is to point to Christ (15:6).

The woman at the well was a witness and apparently an effective one, because John 4:41 indicates that many others believed. Many who will never believe any preacher can be influenced by the witness of the man in the street. Jesus is Lord of the rush hour and the dissatisfied customer and the lathe and the football field and the dirty dishes. At all times and in all places, we are His witnesses.

During the course of this conversation Jesus and the woman spoke of many subjects. They talked about husbands and water and Jacob and God, also about something for which the hour had come (4:23). Hopefully, the hour has now come for something in our lives. The hour has come for commitment. Let us not say we shall do it in four months (4:35). Let us not wait until we can straighten out our lives. Let us not wait for a husband or wife to decide with us. For our decision, the hour has come and now is. If ours is the "now generation," let it be the "now generation" for God.

In the Gospel of John there are two occasions when Jesus spoke about His thirst. One was at Jacob's well (4:7). The second was as Jesus was dying on the cross. One of His seven words from the cross was His cry "I thirst" (19:28). Is that your cry and my cry today? I thirst!

I thirst, not for physical water but for spiritual water.

I thirst, not for Jacob's water but for Jesus' water.

I thirst, not for a diet drink but for a divine drink.

I thirst, not for liquid but for life.

I thirst, not in my mouth but for my Master.

I thirst, not for the ordinary but for the extraordinary.

I thirst, not to satiate salivary glands but to satiate salvation glands,

I thirst, not for pleasure but for paradise.

I thirst, not for the bitter waters of Marah but for the better waters of God.

I thirst, not for stormy waters but for still waters and the still small voice.

I thirst, not for a cup but for Christ.

I thirst, not for a glass but for God.

8

Take Christmas with You

"On the original Christmas tree, the gift was nailed to the tree."—William J. Lacy

Introduction

When I was two years old, my family moved from our first home in Lauderdale County, Mississippi, to Tallapoosa County, Alabama. When I was four, we then moved to Wetumpka, Alabama. When I was six it was McRae, Georgia; at thirteen it was Ravanel, South Carolina. During those years, as long as my grandparents were living, my parents and I would return to Mississippi for Christmas. My parents would pack the presents in the car, and in a sense we would take Christmas with us.

In a profoundly spiritual way, taking Christmas with us has the wisdom of a divine mandate. At Christmas we listen to choirs singing the songs of angels. We follow stars with wise men. We appreciate peace on earth, good will toward men. We should never let it end on Christmas day. Take Christmas with you!

After the shepherds had found Jesus in the stable, Luke 2:20 records, "And the shepherds went back, glorifying and praising God for all that they had heard and seen, just as had been told them." It sounds as if they took Christmas with them. Any person who goes back—back to his flocks, his family, his business, his classes, his responsibilities, his burdens, his crosses, his disappointments, his thorns, while glorifying and praising God, takes Christmas with him.

After the wise men had brought their gold, frankincense, and myrrh,

Matthew 2:12 reports, "And having been warned by God in a dream not to return to Herod, they departed for their own country by another way." It sounds as if they took Christmas with them. Anyone who really finds Christ and is found by Him, anyone who offers his best gifts to Him and receives God's unspeakable gift of Him, anyone who listens to King Jesus rather than King Herod, anyone who is warned by God in dreams and who dreams the impossible dream that, by the grace of God, becomes possible, anyone who follows the best light he has is taking Christmas with him.

Anyone who takes Christmas with him always departs another way.

> Before Christmas is sadness; after Christmas is joy.
> Before Christmas is despair; after Christmas is hope.
> Before Christmas is death; after Christmas is life,
> Before Christmas is pride; after Christmas is self-denial.
> Before Christmas is hell; after Christmas is heaven.
> Before Christmas is defeat; after Christmas is victory.
> Before Christmas is frustration; after Christmas is meaning.
> Before Christmas is loneliness; after Christmas is fellowship.
> Before Christmas is darkness; after Christmas is light.
> Before Christmas is separation; after Christmas is salvation.

How Do We Package Christmas?

If we are to take Christmas with us, Christ must also go with us. Doing that is not as easy as it may appear. God is not an object we may put in a box. God is not a pet around whose neck we may fix a collar and lead Him about. God is not an ornament to be fixed on the dash of our cars. God's presence is not assured by wearing some symbol of Him around our necks. God will not be manipulated by magic or prayer or sermon. Packaging Christmas requires incarnational living, which involves our being change agents in a world whose speed is stuck on fast forward. Evelyn Underhill wrote:

> The saints do not stand aside wrapped in delightful prayers, and feeling pure and agreeable to God. They go right down into the mess; and there, right down in the mess, they are able to radiate God because they possess

Him. And that, above all else, is the priestly work that wins and heals souls.[2]

Bill McFatter is a faithful deacon in the First Baptist Church of Lake Charles. Before his retirement he served as a pilot who guided large ships up and down the channel from the Gulf of Mexico to the port of Lake Charles. On Friday, October 29, 1982, Bill called and asked if I would like to go with him as he directed a ship down the channel. I was excited about going. I met him in the port's parking lot at eleven o'clock that morning. We boarded a tugboat named the *Allan*. The tug had an engine configuration that was a twin screw 3,900-horsepower diesel. Captain Guy Maxey sailed us up Contraband Bayou which got its name from the pirate, Jean Lafitte, who supposedly kept some of his contraband near there.

About noon we reached the PPG dock where we boarded a ship called the *Osco Stripe*. The *Osco Stripe* was taking a load of caustic soda to Australia. Two tugboats were there to assist the ship in leaving the dock and beginning its journey down the channel. The *Allan* was one tug, and the *Edith* was the second.

The *Osco Stripe* was 563 feet long and eighty-seven feet wide. The ship had a draft (the area below water) of thirty-seven feet and ten inches. The ship had a loaded weight of 33,950 tons. The channel was forty feet deep and 400 feet wide. On the journey down the channel, Bill would call directions to the quartermaster who stood at the wheel. He would call such directions as midships (rudder on dead center), port twenty, starboard twenty, dead slow, slow, hard port. The channel had a sharp turn just before the ship was to go under the I-210 bridge which is 135 feet above water. At that point Bill gave the command to stop engines, and the two tugboats pushed the bow of the ship around to assist with the turn.

Because of the limited area for navigation, the captain and crew of the *Osco Stripe* were most attentive to the pilot's instructions, and they were diligent in carrying out the commands with prompt dispatch.

Jesus is our pilot. He knows our destination; He knows the turns and shoals that threaten a meaningful voyage. He needs no radar to detect the storms that threaten us. We must let Him set our compass. We must be attentive to His calls for course changes and prompt in carrying out every command with responsible dispatch. Such obedience will make every day Christmas.

If we are to be with Christ, we must go with Him. Like the wise men, we must follow the best light we have. It may be the light of God's Word or the light of love, but we must follow it even unto Bethlehem. In following, as Martin Luther discovered, we find God in unusual places.[3] God in a stable, God at the breast of Mary, God at a carpenter's bench, God on a cross. Who would expect to find Him there?

If we are to take Christmas with us, Christ must remain central in our thinking. "Tell me where you stand on Christ and I will tell you who you are."[4] We need spiritual brain transplants that the same mind (mind-set) may be in us that was also in Christ Jesus.

One detraction from the centrality of Christ could be Santa Claus. Santa Claus is a source of considerable happiness, but the lines should never be blurred between the Savior and Santa. Saint Nick spreads joy but not the joy of our salvation. He brings gifts but not "the" Gift. He fills our stockings, but he does not fill us with the Holy Spirit. His specialty is toys, not twice-born men and women. His means of transport is a sleigh, not the transport of the Spirit. Madison Avenue welcomes his coming, but the Magi do not recognize him. He is familiar with carols but not a cross.

A distraction on the spiritual canvas of our lives could be a Scrooge mentality. Charles Dickens has made immortal a man who was as opposite to the meaning of Christmas as anyone who ever lived. His name was Scrooge. Scrooge was so mean he must have taken meanness pills. He looked so ornery that a face on an iodine bottle would have been an improvement over his. Scrooge was a hard taskmaster who reaped where he had not sown and who gathered where he had not strawed. Scrooge was a conniving, tight-fisted, grasping, covetous old sinner. Ebenezer Scrooge's answer to a merry Christmas was "Humbug!"

In becoming greedy getters we make Christmas excess baggage. As Wordsworth lamented:

> The world is too much with us; late and soon,
> Getting and spending, we lay waste our powers:
> Little we see in Nature that is ours;
> We have given our hearts away; a sordid boon.[5]

In his book, *The Healing of Persons,* Dr. Paul Tournier wrote:

> Creative imagination, calm thought, artistic production, the gentle things
> of life, the things of the heart and the soul have been strangled in this race to
> achieve and produce more and more. And humanity has no idea what to do
> with all its material wealth and all the products of its activity. It suffers from
> sterility amidst its granaries. It has looked for profits and can no longer
> even sell. For in a civilization in which action and technical progress have
> become the norm, money is king, and material return the only criterion of
> value.[6]

Schedules that are too frantic have no time for the Lord of time. Too
many are the sons of Martha, cumbered by things, when the one needful
mien is to sit at Jesus' feet. Vance Havner said, "I am convinced that if
the devil cannot make us lazy, he will make us so busy here and there that
the best is sacrificed for the good."[7] We need to pray, "Slow me down,
Lord." We should smell the roses and become sacrifices with a fragrant
aroma pleasing to God.

Sin certainly blights Christmas. Whatever became of sin? It is alive
and well! The account of its death has been greatly exaggerated. We
invent pleasant euphemisms for our sins. We exorcise the word from our
vocabularies. We rationalize it. We redefine it. We institutionalize sin.
We legalize it and give it respectability. It remains an unholy holocaust
whose fallout comes as a pallbearer to all that is high and holy.

In the shoes of sin, the soldiers of Herod are always at our gates ready
to kill the children of Christmas. We must keep Christ central in our
lives.

Take Christmas with you. Let Christ be Immanuel, "God with us."
Let love find an incarnation in us. David H. C. Read has told about the
Christmas he spent in 1941.[8] He was a POW in a German prison camp
located in a race track near Rouen, France. About a thousand prisoners,

mostly disabled, were confined there. There had been a little hope that they might be "home for Christmas." Instead, they learned that they were to be shipped across Europe to the border of Poland.

Inside, prisoners were trying to keep warm. Outside, sentries were trying to do the same. Read indicated that for a couple of days a miracle happened. The German commander had brought into the camp a large Christmas tree. The prisoners prepared an elaborate Christmas card which was presented to the commander one midnight. One of the prisoners took some weak cocoa to a shivering guard. One night from one of the huts, a German soldier with a beautiful tenor voice was heard singing "Stille Nacht, Heilige Nacht." They had taken Christmas with them.

The Gifts of Christmas

How do we take Christmas with us? We give gifts year 'round. One little boy had misunderstood the Christmas story, and he told a friend that the wise men gave to Jesus gold, Frankenstein, and Myrtle. A mother was trying to impress the spirit of Christmas on her ten-year old when she said, "Just think, Johnny, many children have no mommy, no daddy, and no Aunt Hattie. Don't you think we could give them something?"

"I suppose we could," answered Johnny. "Let's give them Aunt Hattie."

What are some gifts we may give? Give the gift of friendship. Time and emotional energy are required to offer this gift. I read in our daily paper, *The Lake Charles American Press,* for December 20, 1986, that a certain woman died. She had lived in a remote area of Canada, and she was commonly called "the loneliest woman in the world." Many are lonely who need a friend. Elizabeth Barrett Browning asked Charles Kingsley the secret of his life, and he answered, "I had a friend."[9] Elton Trueblood has written, "As I look back upon the course of my life I realize that my chief wealth has been that of friendship."[10]

The line of a friend is never busy. They accept us as we are, warts and all. Miss Esther Cathy was a radiant, victorious Christian whom I had the privilege of knowing as her pastor. As a child she had polio. In her

own words, "crazy disabling diseases, strange disastrous storms, fright-
ening fires, horrible accidents, frustrating disappointment, financial de-
pressions, deep sorrows, and impossible missions" played havoc with
some of her plans, but she was more than a conqueror.[11] She became a
beloved teacher, a civic-minded citizen, and a leader in her church. With
a ready smile and genuine wit, she had a host of friends.

She has told of receiving a surprise card from her friend Margaret.
The card had on it the appreciative lines:

> There are certain things we can do without
>   And manage to get along
> But to travel through life without a friend
>   Is like never hearing a song
> For a friend is someone who understands
>   And accepts the things we do
> And blessings double when they are shared
>   With a wonderful friend like you.[12]

In his book, *The Christian Pastor,* Dr. Wayne Oates teaches, "The
ministry of friendship is the indispensable necessity for all other deeper
levels of pastoral work. It is the seedbed of most fruitful services to people."[13] How may we have friends? Proverbs 17:17 answers us, "A friend
loves at all times, / and a brother is born for adversity." Proverbs 18:24
adds, "A man of many friends comes to ruin, / But there is a friend who
sticks closer than a brother." Have a listening ear and a strong shoulder.
Don't preach to your friends. Encourage others, and you will have a host
of friends. Giving the gift of friendship means giving yourself.

Give the gift of forgiveness. The Bible has much to say about forgiveness. The psalmist (Ps. 130:4) sang about God, "But there is forgiveness
with thee . . ." David said (Ps. 32:1), "How blessed is he whose trans-
gression is forgiven." In the Lord's Prayer (Matt. 6:12), Jesus taught us
to pray, "And forgive us our debts, as we also have forgiven our
debtors." Jesus practiced what He preached when He prayed from the
cross, "Father, forgive them for they know not what they do." 1 John 1:9
assures us, "If we confess our sins, He is faithful and righteous to for-

give us our sins, and to cleanse us from all unrighteousness." In his book, *The Person Reborn,* Tournier teaches, "Forgiveness is needed in order to love . . ."[14] If we are not forgiving, we are not loving. Warren Wiersbe calls forgiveness "the greatest miracle in the Bible."[15] Sir J. Y. Simpson was asked what he thought his greatest discovery had been, and he answered, "God forgives."[16]

Mankind has solved the problem of polio, smallpox, measles, and energy. They can go through the air like a bird and through the water like a fish. He tries to solve the sin problem. Congress cannot appropriate enough money to solve it. Education cannot solve it. Our works of righteousness cannot solve it. Mankind is morally bankrupt. The only answer is in God's forgiveness.

We must accept forgiveness. Many scholars define forgiveness as the restoration of the sinner to fellowship with God. If this is to happen, forgiveness cannot be one-sided. It must be accepted. There are requirements in this acceptance. One of them is our having a forgiving spirit. We must really forgive. Some may forgive intellectually who do not forgive emotionally. Their facial expressions, their turned backs give them away. We must truly forgive. Paul emphasized that we should forgive each other even as God for Christ's sake has forgiven us.

A lot of forgiveness is required in marriage. I know marriages where there have been financial adversity, physical abuse, alcoholism, sexual unfaithfulness, nervous breakdowns, and extended stays in mental hospitals, yet the couple found genuine love for each other. Their love became exciting, caring, respecting, and responsible. Their relationship was not a truce. It was not a cease-fire. It was not an endurance contest for the sake of the kids. Their love was real. The wife could scarcely wait until her husband came home from work, and the husband could scarcely wait until he was able to affirm his love.

That kind of relationship cannot be when one mate provides instant replays of every sin the other ever committed. We must forgive in reality, and that may be agonizingly hard. Who can stand at the foot of the cross and pretend that forgiveness comes easily? It does not!

Christmas should be a time of giving and forgiving. At Christmas we put on our presents a sticker that has the words "Do Not Open Until Christmas." Spiritually, there are gifts that will never be opened until Christ is born in our hearts, and one such gift is forgiveness.

Give the gift of faithfulness. Don't be a Christmas and Easter Christian. Be faithful in season and out. Be in your place. Be responsible. A little boy was bragging on his horse one day, and his friend said, "Aw, Billy, that old nag can't run fast."

"No," said Billy, "but he can stand fast."

Can you live the role of Bunyan's Mister Standfast? For five years I was Red Davis's pastor in the First Baptist Church of Hapeville, Georgia. Red and his wife lived on Central Avenue. Red was a carpenter. On Sunday mornings Red was usually the first member at church. On Easter Sunday, 1988, Red completed fifty years of perfect attendance in Sunday School. What a record! It is a tremendous achievement in any generation but is especially remarkable in our mobile society. Think of the numerous teachers he had, the many discussions on various lessons, the changes in literature, the reorganization of the Sunday School, the various pastors, the occasional severe weather.

Didn't Red ever get sick? Didn't Red want to go to family reunions? Didn't Red take vacations? Whatever he wanted or did, he was always in his place. May his tribe increase! I don't have a record like that of Red Davis, but I wish I did. God said to the church at Smyrna, ". . . be thou faithful unto death, and I will give thee a crown of life" (Rev. 2:10). Jesus taught, "He that is faithful in that which is least is faithful also in much" (Luke 16:10).

Keep "the" Christmas Tree in Place

Take Christmas with you! How do you do it? You keep "the" Christmas tree in place all year. What tree is that? It is the accursed tree, the cross, the only tree the Bible relates to Christ, the tree on which Christ died for you and me. Out of World War II came a heroic story about a young captain who saw a sergeant severely wounded.[17] The captain crawled onto the battlefield and pulled the sergeant to safety. As he was dragging him in from the range of bullets, the captain was hit and later died from the wound. The sergeant, however, recovered and went home. Later, the sergeant was invited to a meal at the home of the captain's parents. The sergeant arrived late. When he arrived he was half drunk, and throughout the meal he was ill-mannered. After a delicious meal he left quickly without even mentioning the captain's bravery in saving his life. When he had gone, the mother began to weep and said to her husband, "To think that our son had to die to save a thing like that!"

I wonder if God ever looks at the garbage that constitutes our lives and says, "To think that my Son had to die to save a thing like that!"

To take Christmas with you, keep the cross in your life. We should have a similar view to P. T. Forsyth who regarded the cross as the center of history, the key to Christian ethics, and the clue to God's final dealings with the world.[18] H. Wheeler Robinson believed that through the Holy Spirit, the cross was transformed for Paul "from the wooden instrument of a dreamer's death to the supreme altar of the Christian faith."[19] Luther was right; Christianity is a *theologia crucis,* a theology of the cross.

A new theological emphasis in recent years has been a system called "theology of hope." Jurgen Moltmann wrote, "Theology of hope is at its hard core theology of the cross."[20] The cross needs to be the hard core of everything. Not long before Walter Rauschenbusch died, he gave his last lecture. To make the asking of questions easier, they were written on slips of paper and passed to him. The first question was, "What does the church need today?" The quick reply was, "The restoration of the cross."[21]

We Christians tend to glamorize the agony in Jesus' life. We overlook the details that were not so pleasant, the fact that the world had no room for Him, that He came unto His own and His own received Him not, that He was born in a stable. The stable could have been a cave, but whatever it was, it did not have wall-to-wall carpet, central heating, or hot and cold running water. It was not located adjacent to the Bethlehem Baptist Hospital with all the up-to-date facilities for delivering babies. It is easy to forget the cold, the dirt, the drabness, the inconvenience, the stench.

We view Jesus' ministry in a similar vein. We marvel at the miracles. We memorize His powerful words. We forget the fact that people doubted His signs, and in the end, few listened to His words. We minimize the dusty roads and the nights when the Son of Man had nowhere to lay His head. We put on our rose-colored glasses when considering His frustrations and disappointments, such as some family members thinking He was daft, or disciples who were slow to learn, or one disciple who denied knowing Him, and another who betrayed Him. The preachers were always questioning His authority or His teachings or His healing on the sabbath.

In a similar spirit, we can take an unrealistic view of what happened on Calvary. By design the cross was the ultimate in pain and humiliation. In the first century it was a scandal for a person to worship someone who had been crucified.

The meaning of the cross should be vitally relevant today. It should influence decisions at the State Department and in the board rooms of corporations and in relationships to the kid next door. Cross-bearing is not exclusively for those with extreme problems. It is not only for the husband whose wife is an invalid or for the wife whose husband is an alcoholic or for the parents with a delinquent child. To bear one's cross means to accept one's Christian responsibility of living by the principle of the cross. Amy Carmichael spoke to the contemporary scene when she wrote:

> We grovel among trifles and our spirits
> fret and toss.
> And above us burns the vision of the
> Christ upon the cross.[22]

Take Christmas with you. Keep in view "the" accursed Christmas tree. Decorate that tree biblically. Remember, the cross has:

> one ornament—the man who died on it;
> one light—the man who died on it;
> one gift—the man who died on it;
> one shepherd—the man who died on it;
> one conclusion—that of the Roman Centurion: "Surely
> this man was the Son of God";

one result—the forgiveness of sins;

one message—"God was in Christ reconciling the world
    unto Himself";

one foundation—the love of God;

one power—the power of God unto salvation;

one life—abundant, eternal life;

one blood stain—the blood that flowed from royal arteries;

one priest—the priest greater than Melchizedek;

one prophet—the prophet greater than Moses;

one king—the king no one wanted;

one wisdom—the wisdom of God;

one *post mortem*—the resurrection;

one hope—the hope of the world;

one funeral—the death of death;

one claim—God's claim on you;

one mystery—the mystery hidden with Christ in God;

one vision—that every knee should bow and every
    tongue confess that Jesus is Lord to the glory
    of God the Father;

one glory—the glory of the only begotten of the
    Father, full of grace and truth;

one peace—the peace that passeth all understanding;

one responsibility—to take it up and live by it;

one question—will you accept it?

Notes

Preface

1. Wayne E. Oates, *The Struggle to Be Free* (Philadelphia: The Westminster Press, 1983), p. 161.

2. George A. Buttrick, *The Parables of Jesus* (Grand Rapids: Baker Book House, 1928), p. XXIII.

Chapter 1

1. S. D. Gordon, *Quiet Talks on Prayer* (New York: Grosset & Dunlap, 1941), p. 16.

2. Joachim Jeremias, *The Prayers of Jesus* (Philadelphia: Fortress Press, 1967), p. 78.

3. E. F. Hallock, *Always in Prayer* (Nashville: Broadman Press, 1966), p. 15.

4. Charles G. Finney, *Revivals of Religion* (Virginia Beach, Virginia: CBN University Press, 1978), p. 119.

5. Robert G. Lee, *Glory Today for Conquest Tomorrow* (Orlando, Florida: Christ For The World Publishers, n.d.), p. 13.

6. Elie Wiesel, *Souls On Fire* (New York: Summit Books, 1972), p. 49.

7. Harry Emerson Fosdick, *What Is Vital in Religion* (New York: Harper & Row, 1955), p. 9.

8. John Bartlett, *Familiar Quotations* (Boston: Little, Brown, & Co., 1968), p. 1,004.

9. Thomas Brooks, "God's Perspective," *The New Pulpit Digest*, LII, 399 (Jan.-Feb., 1973), p. 13.

10. James S. Stewart, *The Wind of the Spirit* (Nashville: Abingdon Press, 1968), p. 133.

11. *The World's Great Religious Poetry*. Caroline Miles Hill, ed. (N.Y.: The Macmillan Co., 1943), p. 410.

12. James W. English, *Handyman of the Lord: The Life and Ministry of The Reverend William Holmes Borders* (New York: Meredith Press, 1967), p. 6.

13. Karl Barth, *Church Dogmatics*, III, Part 4: *The Doctrine of Creation* (Edinburgh: T. & T. Clark, 1961), p. 88.

14. Wes Seeliger, *One Inch from the Fence* (Atlanta: Forum House, 1973), p. 16.

15. Karl Barth, *Church Dogmatics,* III, Part 4: *The Doctrine of Creation* (Edinburgh: T. & T. Clark, 1961), p. 88.

16. Michael Downey, "Worship Between the Holocausts," *Theology Today,* XLIII, 1 (April, 1986), p. 75.

17. Harry Emerson Fosdick, *The Meaning of Prayer* (Nashville: Abingdon Press, 1962), p. 78.

18. E. M. Bounds, *Power Through Prayer* (Grand Rapids: Zondervan Publishing House, 1974), p. 26.

19. E. Stanley Jones, *The Way* (New York: Abingdon-Cokesbury Press, 1946), p. 209.

20. S. D. Gordon, *Quiet Talks on Prayer* (New York: Grosset & Dunlap, 1941), pp. 10-11.

21. *Ibid.,* pp. 12-13.

22. Dorothea S. Kopplin, *Something to Live By* (Garden City: Garden City Books, 1945), p. 73.

Chapter 2

1. Dorothea S. Kopplin, *Ibid.,* p. 70.

2. Heard in one of his sermons.

3. Henlee H. Barnette, *Exploring Medical Ethics* (Macon, Georgia: Mercer University Press, 1982), p. 44.

4. Billy Graham, "We Set Forth the Truth Plainly," *Preaching,* I, 1 (July-Aug., 1985), p. 4.

5. Charles R. Swindoll, *Growing Strong in the Seasons of Life* (Portland: Multnomah Press, 1983), p. 337.

6. Soren Kierkegaard, *The Sickness Unto Death* (Garden City: Doubleday and Co., Inc., 1954), p. 143.

7. Gerald Kennedy, "The Starting Line," *Pulpit Digest,* LII, 394 (April, 1972), p. 58.

8. Harold E. Dye, *No Rocking Chair for Me!* (Nashville: Broadman Press, 1975), p. 44.

9. Elton Trueblood, *The Future of the Christian* (New York: Harper & Row Publishers, 1971), pp. 34-35.

10. Wayne Dehoney, "Lord, Make Us More Thinkful," *Pulpit Digest,* XLVI, 326 (Nov., 1965), p. 33.

11. William A. Jones, *God in the Ghetto* (Elgin, Illinois: Progressive Baptist Publishing House, 1979), p. 149.

12. Leon F. Litwack, *Been in the Storm So Long* (New York: Vintage Books, 1979), p. VII.

13. Douglas M. White, *Vance Havner: Journey from Jugtown* (Old Tappan, New Jersey: F. H. Revell Co., 1977), p. 136.

14. Paul W. Powell, *The Nuts and Bolts of Church Growth* (Nashville: Broadman Press, 1982), p. 24.

15. Richard Cecil, *The Life of the Rev. John Newton* (Grand Rapids: Baker Book House, 1978), p. 214.

16. Harold W. Kaser, "Pilgrims of the Road," *Pulpit Digest* (Feb., 1971), p. 13.

17. Archibald MacLeish, *J. B.* (New York: S. French, 1958), p. 13.

18. "Points to Ponder," *Reader's Digest,* Vol. 124, No. 745 (May, 1984), p. 169.

Chapter 3

1. Esther Cathy, *Under His Wings* (Macon, Georgia: Omni Publishers, 1982), p. 3.

2. C. Roy Angell, *Iron Shoes* (Nashville: Broadman Press, 1953), p. 30.

3. W. E. Sangster, *Can I Know God?* (Grand Rapids: Baker Book House, 1960), p. 55.

4. Samuel J. Stone, "The Church's One Foundation," *Baptist Hymnal* (Nashville: Convention Press, 1975), p. 236.

5. Billy Graham, *World Aflame* (Garden City: Doubleday & Co., Inc., 1965), p. 13.

6. Nicholas Bentley, "Thoughts," *Think* (July-Aug., 1964), p. 28.

7. Robert C. Leslie, *Jesus and Logotherapy* (N.Y.: Abingdon Press, 1965), p. 93.

8. Roger Lovette, "A Monument to Misery," *Pulpit Digest,* I, 369 (Nov., 1969), p. 24.

9. Howard C. Schenk, "Ruth's Reward," *Open Windows,* XXX, 4 (Nashville: The Sunday School Board of the Southern Baptist Convention), Friday, October 21, 1966.

10. George Matheson, "O Love That Wilt Not Let Me Go," *Baptist Hymnal* (Nashville: Convention Press, 1975), p. 368.

11. G. Campbell Morgan, *The Practice of Prayer* (Grand Rapids: Baker Book House, 1971), p. 99.

12. Karl Barth, *The Word Of God and the Word of Man* (New York: Harper & Bros. Publishers, 1957), p. 92.

13. David Mace, *Love and Anger in Marriage* (Grand Rapids: Zondervan Publishing House, 1982), p. 71.

14. *The Journal of John Wesley,* Percy Livingstone Parker, editor (Chicago: Moody Press, n.d.), p. 61.

15. Vance Havner, *Don't Miss Your Miracle* (Grand Rapids: Baker Book House, 1984), p. 16.

Chapter 4

1. Jack Gulledge, *Ideas and Illustrations for Inspirational Talks* (Nashville: Broadman Press, 1986), p. 44.

2. W. L. Lumpkin, *Baptist Confessions of Faith* (Chicago: The Judson Press, 1959), p. 365.

3. T. Cecil Myers, *You Can Be More Than You Are* (Waco: Word Books, 1976), p. 45.

4. G. A. Studdert-Kennedy, "Builders," *The Unutterable Beauty: The Collected Poetry of G. A. Studdert-Kennedy* (London: Hodder and Stoughton, 1927), p. 127.

5. Paul Scherer, *For We Have This Treasure* (Grand Rapids: Baker Book House, 1944), p. 178.

6. James Allen, *As a Man Thinketh* (London: Collins, 1967), p. 51.

7. "Starting Point," *Pulpit Digest*, LIII, 402 (July-Aug., 1973), p. 32.

8. J. Estill Jones, "The New Testament and Southern," *Review And Expositor*, LXXXII, 1 (Winter, 1985), p. 23.

9. Dewey M. Beegle, *Scripture, Tradition, and Infallibility* (Grand Rapids: William B. Eerdmans Publishing Co., 1973), p. 18.

10. Lesslie Newbigin, *The Household of God* (New York: Friendship Press, 1953), p. 25.

11. Karl Barth, *The Epistle to the Romans* (London: Oxford University Press, 1957), p. 3.

12. Timothy George, "Systematic Theology at Southern Seminary," *Review And Expositor*, LXXXII, 1 (Winter, 1985), p. 44.

13. Jurgen Moltmann, *The Experiment Hope* (Philadelphia: Fortress Press, 1975), p. 3.

14. Vance Packard, *The Status Seekers* (New York: Pocket Books, Inc., 1959), p. 171.

15. Delores Elaine Bius, "Do It Today," *Home Life*, Vol. 39, No. 2 (Nashville: The Sunday School Board of The Southern Baptist Convention, November, 1982), p. 43.

16. Dag Hammarskjold, *Markings* (New York: Alfred A. Knopf, 1965), p. 91.

17. David H. C. Read, "The Churches Under Fire," *Pulpit Digest*, XLVIII, 353 (April, 1968), p. 11.

18. Veronica Zundel (ed.), *Famous Prayers* (Grand Rapids: Wm. B. Eerdmans Publ. Co., 1983), p. 23.

19. Charles L. Allen, *The Touch of The Master's Hand* (Westwood, N.J.: Fleming H. Revell Co., 1956), p. 77.

20. Vance Havner, *Pepper 'N Salt* (Westwood, N.J.: Fleming H. Revell Co., 1966), p. 80.

21. Winston S. Churchill, *The Grand Alliance* (Boston: Houghton Mifflin Co., 1951), p. 26.

22. *The Atlanta Constitution* (newspaper), Tuesday, January 15, 1974, p. 6-B.

23. F. Deaville Walker, *William Carey: Missionary Pioneer And Statesman* (Chicago: Moody Press, 1960), p. 42.

Chapter 5

1. Paul Tournier, *Guilt and Grace* (New York: Harper & Row, 1962), p. 57.

2. Hugh T. Kerr and John M. Mulder (eds.), *Conversions* (Grand Rapids: William B. Eerdmans Publishing Co., 1983), p. 145.

3. Karl Menninger, *Whatever Became of Sin?* (New York: Hawthorn Books, Inc., 1973), p. 13.

4. *The Best of John H. Jowell* (Grand Rapids: Baker Book House, 1981), p. 25.

5. Karl Barth, *Church Dogmatics* III/3 (Edinburgh: T. & T. Clark, 1960), p. 90.

6. Walker L. Knight, "In the Image of Love," *Missions USA,* Vol. 53, No. 6 (Nov.-Dec., 1982), p. 3.

7. Johnstone G. Patrick, "Gafia," *Pulpit Digest,* LII, 392 (Feb., 1972), p. 36.

8. *The Book of Common Prayer,* Ratified in 1789 (New York: The Church Pension Fund, 1945), p. 67.

9. Robert L. Short, *The Parables of Peanuts* (New York: Harper & Row Publishers, 1968), p. 53.

10. Rollo May, *Psychology and the Human Dilemma* (Princeton, N.J.: D. Van Nostrand Company, Inc., 1967), p. 133.

11. A. F. Kirkpatrick, *The Book of Psalms* (Cambridge: University Press, 1951), p. 785.

12. George Arthur Buttrick, *Prayer* (New York: Abingdon-Cokesbury Press, 1942), p. 215.

13. Dick Eastman, *The Hour That Changes the World* (Grand Rapids: Baker Book House, 1978), p. 142.

14. Gerald Kennedy, "The Starting Line," *Pulpit Digest* LII, 387 (Sept., 1971), p. 60.

15. J. E. Dillard, *Good Stewards* (Nashville: Broadman Press, 1953), p. 38.

Chapter 6

1. Esther Cathy, *Under His Wings* (Macon, Georgia: Omni Publishers, 1982), p. 112.

2. Donald K. McKim (ed.), *How Karl Barth Changed My Mind* (Grand Rapids: William B. Eerdmans Publishing Co., 1986), p. 39.

3. Bernard Ramm, *Offense to Reason* (San Francisco: Harper & Row, Publishers, 1985), p. 23.

4. Wes Seeliger, *One Inch from the Fence* (Atlanta: Forum House Publishers, 1973), p. 16.

5. Robert G. Lee, *Pulpit Pleadings* (Nashville: Broadman Press, 1948), p. 17.

6. John Bartlett, *Familiar Quotations* (Boston: Little, Brown, & Co., 1968), p. 454.

7. Douglas M. White, *Vance Havner: Journey from Jugtown* (Old Tappan, N.J.: F. H. Revell Co., 1977), p. 158.

8. Clovis G. Chappell, *More Sermons on Biblical Characters* (N.Y.: George H. Doran Co., 1923), p. 180.

9. T. Cecil Myers, *You Can Be More Than You Are* (Waco: Word Books, Publishers, 1976), p. 18.

10. Hardy R. Denham, Jr., "Getting Ready For Easter," *Proclaim,* Vol. 14, No. 2 (Jan.-Mar. 1984), p. 9.

11. Roy L. Smith, *Sidewalk Sermons* (New York: Abingdon-Cokesbury, 1938), p. 23.

12. Robert G. Lee, *Pulpit Pleadings* (Nashville: Broadman Press, 1948), p. 178.

13. Earl Waldrup, *New Church Member Orientation Manual* (Nashville: Convention Press, 1905), p. 3.

14. Gaines S. Dobbins, *Evangelism According to Christ* (Nashville: Broadman Press, 1949), p. 94.

15. Ernest Stoeffler (ed.), *Continental Pietism and Early American Christianity* (Grand Rapids: William B. Eerdmans Publishing Co., 1976), p. 81.

16. William Deal, *John Bunyan: The Tinker of Bedford* (Westchester, Illinois: Good News Publishers, 1977), p. 10.

17. Marvin W. Kanengieter and Edith Quinlan, *Looking At Life's Relationships* (Denver: Accent-B/P Publishers, 1979), p. 24.

18. W. Wayne Price, "Resources for Special Occasions," *Proclaim,* Vol. 14, No. 1 (Oct.-Dec. 1983), p. 44.

19. Herbert C. Eggleston, "Faith at the Interface," *Pulpit Digest,* XLVIII, 356 (July-Aug., 1968), p. 18.

20. James A. Stewart, *The Phenomena of Pentecost* (Alexandria, Louisiana: Lamplighter Publications, n.d.), p. 55.

21. Donald G. Miller, "Deliverance and Destiny," *Interpretation,* IX, 4 (Oct., 1955), p. 416.

22. John Newton, "Amazing Grace! How Sweet the Sound," *Baptist Hymnal* (Nashville: Convention Press, 1975), p. 165.

23. John H. Elliott, "Salutation and Exhortation to Christian Behavior On The Basis of God's Blessings (1:1-2:10)," *Review and Expositor,* LXXIX, 3 (Summer, 1982), p. 418.

Chapter 7

1. John Bartlett, *Familiar Quotations* (Boston: Little, Brown, and Co., 1968), p. 717.

2. Eric Marshall and Stuart Hample (compilers), *Children's Letters to God* (N.Y.: P B Special, 1966), p. 14.

3. James L. Blevins, "Woman's Role in First-Century Judaism," *Biblical Illustrator,* Vol. 9, No. 4 (Summer, 1983), p. 70.

4. William E. Hull, "Woman in Her Place," *Review and Expositor,* LXXII, 1 (Winter, 1975), p. 10.

5. Carlyle Marney, *Structures of Prejudice* (New York: Abingdon Press, 1961), p. 148.

6. *Ibid.,* p. 157.

7. This statement was made by Rabbi Feibelman in a seminary class taught by Dr. Penrose St. Amant.

8. James L. Sullivan, *Reach Out!* (Nashville: Broadman Press, 1970), p. 118.

9. Jerry W. Mixon, *Off the Main Road* (Nashville: Broadman Press, 1985), p. 77.

10. Tim LaHaye, *How to Be Happy Though Married* (Wheaton, Illinois: Tyndale House Publishers, 1968), p. 41.

11. Franklin M. Segler, *Christian Worship* (Nashville: Broadman Press, 1967), pp. 83-84.

12. Edward L. R. Elson, "News from the Cemetery," *Pulpit Digest,* I, 373 (March, 1970), p. 34.

Chapter 8

1. Brewer L. Burnett, "The Need for Courage," *Pulpit Digest,* XLV, 318 (Feb., 1965), p. 13.

2. Carl Michalson, *The Hinge of History* (N.Y.: Charles Scribner's Sons, 1959), p. 164.

3. Jaroslav Pelikan, "Jesus Christ Through the Centuries: His Place in the History of Culture," *Theology Today,* XLIII, 1 (April, 1986), p. 102.

4. Roy J. Cook (Comp.), *One Hundred and One Famous Poems* (Chicago: Contemporary Books, Inc., 1958), p. 64.

5. Paul Tournier, *The Healing of Persons* (San Francisco: Harper & Row, 1965), p. 73.

6. Vance Havner, *The Best of Vance Havner* (Grand Rapids: Baker Book House, 1969), p. 37.

7. David H. C. Read, *Sons of Anak* (New York: Charles Scribner, 1964), pp. 79-80.

8. A. E. Prince, *Life's Best* (Kansas City: Western Baptist Publishing Co., 1940), p. 15.

9. D. Elton Trueblood, *Essays In Gratitude* (Nashville: Broadman Press, 1982), p. 20.

10. Esther Cathy, *Under His Wings* (Macon: Mercer Press Services, 1982), p. 2.

11. *Ibid.,* p. 288.

12. Wayne E. Oates, *The Christian Pastor* (Philadelphia: The Westminster Press, 1982), p. 196.

13. Paul Tournier, *The Person Reborn* (New York: Harper & Row, 1966), p. 36.

14. Billy Graham, *How to Be Born Again* (Waco: Word Books, 1977), p. 84.

15. David A MacLennan, "How to Cancel Our Failures," *Pulpit Digest,* XLIII, 297 (Mar., 1963), p. 26.

16. "No Price Too High," *Dynamic Preaching,* I, 9 (Sept., 1986), p. 2.

17. A. M. Hunter, *P. T. Forsyth* (Philadelphia: The Westminster Press, 1974), p. 39.

18. H. Wheeler Robinson, *The Christian Experience of the Holy Spirit* (N.Y.: Harper & Bros., 1928), p. 78.

19. Jurgen Moltmann, *The Experiment Hope* (Philadelphia: Fortress Press, 1975), pp. 57-58.

20. R. G. Lee, *Grapes from Gospel Vines* (Nashville: Broadman Press, 1976), p. 144.

21. Amy Carmichael, *Gold Cord* (New York: The Macmillan Co., 1933), p. 9.